7 95

Toronto

by

GEORGE BRYANT

PASSPORT BOOKS
a division of *NTC Publishing Group*
Lincolnwood, Illinois USA

Published by Passport Books, a division of NTC Publishing Group, 4255 West Touhy Avenue, Lincolnwood (Chicago), Illinois 60646–1975 U.S.A.

The contents of this publication are believed correct at the time of printing. Nevertheless, the publishers cannot accept responsibility for errors or omissions, nor for changes in details given. We are always grateful to readers who let us know of any errors or omissions they come across, and future printings will be updated accordingly.

Published by Passport Books in conjunction with The Automobile Association of Great Britain.

Written by George Bryant
"Peace and Quiet" section by Paul Sterry

Library of Congress Catalog
Card Number 93–85607
ISBN 0–8442–8936–1

10 9 8 7 6 5 4 3 2 1

PRINTED IN TRENTO, ITALY

Front cover picture: CN Tower

The weather chart displayed on **page 95** of this book is calibrated in °C and millimetres. For conversion to °F and inches simply use the following formula:

$$25 \cdot 4mm = 1 \text{ inch} \qquad °F = 1 \cdot 8 \times °C + 32$$

This book employs a
simple rating system to
help choose which
places to visit:

◆◆◆   do not miss

◆◆   see if you can

◆   worth seeing if
      you have time

Toronto's skyline, dominated by the CN Tower, on the shores of Lake Ontario. The lakefront setting makes it a metropolis with something of a seaside atmosphere

INTRODUCTION

'Toronto is New York run by the Swiss.'
Peter Ustinov, 1986

Metropolitan Toronto is that rarity among major North American cities — a community of many small-town virtues and few big-city vices, with trees to balance the skyscrapers and racoons in its ravines. It has all the advantages of a city of three million, an art world, theatre, television production, 5,000 restaurants, major-league baseball, hockey and football and that ultimate symbol of sporting prominence, a domed stadium, yet its crime rate is negligible and its downtown full of life.

In Toronto people live in the heart of the city as well as the suburbs and stroll its leafy streets day or night not only with impunity but with pleasure, a state of affairs which may not be all that remarkable in Europe but is almost unknown in major western hemisphere communities.

It is a likeable city, despite being a jumble of office towers, apartment buildings and family homes interspersed with churches, statues, the odd fountain and solemn public buildings, all sprawled out along the north shore of Lake Ontario in the province of Ontario and all dominated by the high-reaching, 1,815ft (553m) spire of the Canadian National Railways television tower, which adds a futuristic cast to the lakefront skyline.

For one thing, the city is clean and free of graffiti, not depressingly so but more like Scandinavia than London, Paris or New York. And things run on time and people queue up politely. And though they are not folksy in the manner of, say, Moscow residents, who have a village chattiness and peasant humour that yields nothing to the competition of big-city life, Torontonians do not have the hard veneer of New York or Chicago residents. What they do have is Presbyterian reticence, inherited from the Scots pioneers of the new land, that can be broken down with one friendly question or a passing smile. Then, like small-town people everywhere, they are quick with advice and help.

To European visitors it is all very American, with gun-toting police, big cars, bars instead of pubs and a careless disregard of distance — workers in the same office may live 60 miles (95km) apart and routinely drive a 120-mile (190km) round-trip to visit each other of an evening. To Americans it is very British, with its King Street, York Street, Queen's Park (the site

It may not have the grandeur of some cities, but it is a pleasant blend of older buildings (above, Old City Hall) and modern tower blocks

of the provincial legislature), neat and liveable downtown, profusion of teapots (the US cup of tea is full of lukewarm water with a bag at the side) and British pronunciations (herbs, not 'erbs and a definite Scots' 'oot' and 'aboot' sound when going out and about).

It is, in fact, a fine blend of the two, the best of both worlds, in a way, with a British heritage, but moulded and amended by the American experience. And that is true in language, schools, government, right through the whole fabric of society. There are lots of fish and chip shops in Toronto, for instance, but you get ketchup with your vinegar and your chips are called French fries. And at the other end of the

scale, if you go to court you will find crown attorneys and Queen's Counsels — but all of them will be North American-style lawyers combining the functions of barristers and solicitors.

With all its attributes, though, Toronto is not a city of grandeur, no London, Paris, Lisbon or Buenos Aires. It grew up on the pioneer ruts of Muddy York's narrow streets and has few sweeping prospects or grand boulevards. Most downtown thoroughfares are dully commercial and Yonge Street, the city's heart, is commonplace where it is not tawdry, lined with raucous bars and record stores and fast food outlets. Only the 12-block length of University Avenue leading north from Front Street to the solemn bulk of the legislative buildings at Queen's Park has any sense of style and occasion. And unfortunately, despite its breadth, central boulevard and sweeping prospect, the street is dull.

There are areas of the city that have that sense of style but they are mostly residential neighbourhoods which came into being as the city grew, areas such as Rosedale and Forest Hill where huge old mansions slumber beside shady streets. For anyone with an interest in architecture and residential beauty these are communities to visit.

The area known to the world as Toronto is, of course, actually five cities and a borough, four of the six with names transported from Britain (York, North York, East York and Scarborough) and two with names of North American origin (the original Toronto and Etobicoke), the whole spread over a 25-mile (40km) stretch of Lake Ontario shoreline 90 miles (145km) from Niagara Falls and the US border. Though each community has its own government for local matters, all work together collectively as Metropolitan Toronto. (It should be noted that some, though by no means all, Torontonians pronounce the name 'Traana' but you will be understood if you say a proper 'Toronto'.)

It sprawls over fairly flat land, with no spectacular hills except at Scarborough Bluffs in the east, where 330ft (100m) cliffs offer a lookout which takes in many waves but no hint of the far shore (not surprisingly, since the lake is from 30 to 53 miles (48 to 85km) wide). But three major rivers, the Humber, the Credit and the Don, as well as numerous creeks and ravines, twist and turn through the urban areas, bringing a breath of the country with their plants and waters and wildlife, which includes racoons as well as rabbits, foxes, squirrels and birds of all descriptions. Add that effect to Toronto's green canopy of trees and its public gardens and you have again a big city that retains small-town touches.

Attractions for visitors are spread right across the 244 square miles (632 sq km) of the metropolitan city, but for most the major lures lie in the downtown area of the original Toronto, at the heart of the community, with its harbour, islands, theatres and concert halls, museums and galleries, hotels, restaurants and shopping.

In the heat of summer (which can run into the 30sC/90sF) it is the waterfront that casts a spell: promenades by the lakeside; harbour tours of every ilk (moonlight cruises, day runs, dinner sailings); ferry rides to Toronto Islands, which rim and protect the harbour, to picnic by the water and drift in canoes down shady lagoons; concerts and hot dogs at Harbourfront and a

The waterfront is an ever-present attraction to visitors, whether for strolling along the lake, joining in the fun at Harbourfront or taking a trip on a ferry to the Islands

stop for a beer and an enveloping Cinesphere
movie at Ontario Place, a wonderland of
domes and towers built out over the water not
far from the site of the first tiny European
settlement, a French fur trading post
established in 1720.

There may be a thousand other things to do in
summer, but put the waterfront high on your list.
And do not overlook it in spring, when a stroll
along Harbourfront's breakwater offers the lift
of fresh lake breezes or in autumn, when the
colour change from the north comes blazing
down the ravines. The change is one of nature's
grandest shows and though it is best seen north
of Toronto (there are bus tours and route maps
for rental car drivers) more than a hint of its
scarlet and yellow glory can be enjoyed right in
the heart of the city.

The city in winter is another matter. The lake
warms the air enough to save Toronto from the
worst of nature's outrages but the bitter winds
and slushy streets and temperatures that can
drop below -17C (0F) tend to send residents
and visitors alike indoors and underground,
where happily they find buried between Yonge
Street and York Street the world's largest
subterranean city, six blocks long by two wide,
three miles (5km) of tunnels with 1,000 shops,
entertainments, bars and restaurants. And,
naturally, this being Toronto, waterfalls,
growing plants and even trees.

And when that palls, if ever, the north end of
the tunnel leads to The Eaton Centre, a
four-block, three-storey complex of shops,
stores, snack bars, restaurants, high-fashion
boutiques, greengrocers and a branch of the
department store whose name it bears. It was
built on the lines of Milan's Galleria purely for
shopping, but the results were so pleasing it
has become a major tourist attraction.

Back in the 1950s the city was known as Toronto
the Good, usually said with some disgust, and
though it is a lot more relaxed now it still could
not be described as wild and woolly. Bars open
at the respectable hour of noon and close at
01.00, you buy liquor at government stores,
Sunday is still a day of rest for most people and
there is no gambling other than on race horses
and lotteries.

The skyscrapers of 20th-century downtown Toronto

That said, it is not dull. West End and Broadway shows play the theatres, restaurants serve the foods of the world, it is a major sports city (though its teams have been in something of a slump recently), your choice in bars is almost unlimited and there are attractions unique to the city, as we shall explore in later chapters. And if cities cramp, then visitors can always trying jogging the length of Yonge Street (pronounced 'young'), the central thoroughfare, though it might take some time. The longest street in the world, it starts at the water's edge and runs north and west as Highway 11 to Rainy River, Ont, on the Minnesota border, a distance of 1,168 miles (1,880km). And all within the province of Ontario.

BACKGROUND

For a city with such a proper image there is an awful lot of rum in Metropolitan Toronto's history; and not a little accident. It sits where it does, for instance, not by choice but by chance. No wise planning went into the decision. It grew up around a British fort that evolved from a British fur trading post that superseded a French trading post that was located at the site of a small Indian village. And the village had straggled into being only because the level piece of ground between the Humber and Don Rivers was the spot where tribes canoeing south from Lake Huron reached Lake Ontario after portaging the lower reaches of the Humber. Down that trail over the centuries had come Hurons and Iroquois, Ottawas and Menominees, Shawanoes and Sacs, Foxes and Mississaugas,

Pioneer's log cabin

war parties and scouts, hunters and nomads, all moving freely in an endless land. And down that trail in early September, 1615, came the young French explorer Etienne Brulé, who lived among the Hurons as a scout for Samuel de Champlain and who spelled the beginning of the end for the natives' free-roving way of life.

He was the first European to see the future site of Toronto, though he was not the man staid city fathers of later years would have chosen for the role. They would have looked for someone combining the courtliness of Sir Walter Raleigh with the holiness of St Francis of Assisi. Brulé was not close on either count. Described as vulgar and barely literate, he brawled and drank and womanised until one drunken quarrel over an Indian maid went too far and he was beaten and eaten by his Huron friends. But that was all far in the future on this day of discovery.

He made no notes and he drew

BACKGROUND

no maps on his visit to the lakeside site the Hurons called Toronto ('meeting place' or 'plenty' in their tongue — we will never know which because the Iroquois wiped them out a few decades later), but he reported back to Champlain and the portage north became a favourite route of such adventurers as La Salle when heading west through the Great Lakes to explore the Mississippi. (It took them to the Holland River, Lake Simcoe, the Severn River, Georgian Bay and Lake Huron, a shortcut that avoided the back-breaking portage at Niagara and the long haul through Lake Erie and upstream against the Detroit River current.)

But while the route was recognised as valuable, the site was not, at least for another century, though somewhat earlier than that some visitors from La Salle's fort at Cataraqui (now Kingston) set the tone for future conventions if not an example for Toronto the Good. The Iroquois Confederacy had moved north into former Huron territory along the shores of Lake Ontario by the late 1670s and some had settled near the mouth of the Humber at a village of typical long houses called Teiaiagon, a tongue-twister of a name that is, happily, long out of use. And among its first European visitors were the men from Cataraqui. What happened then is recorded in a work of the time titled *Histoire de l'eau de vie en Canada:* '. . . Six traders from Katarakuy named Duplessis, Ptolemee, Dautru, Lamouche,

Colin, and Cascaret, made the whole village of Taheyagon drunk, all the inhabitants were dead drunk for three days; the old men, the women and the children got drunk; after which the six traders engaged in the debauch which the savages called Ganuary, running about naked with a keg of brandy under the arm.'

It is hard to understand what lusts that debauch called Ganuary was designed to gratify, other than a desire for an abrupt and noisy end, but the report certainly proves that life on the frontier was not all candle-making and churchgoing.

By 1720, the French had recognised the necessity for a fur trading post at the portage point, if only to intercept Indians on their way to the English traders south of the lake. By 1750 the battle for furs was so intense they replaced the trading post with a proper fort on the east side of the Humber and called it Fort Toronto, the first use of the name for a settlement.

However, it was soon eclipsed by a larger bastion called Fort Rouillé after the colonial minister in Paris (then, as now, one bowed to the powers that be) which briefly flourished as a centre of the fur trade before being set to the torch by its garrison during a British attack in 1759. A single plaque on a stone pillar on the waterfront grounds of the Canadian National Exhibition near Ontario Place marks its site. Little else remains to recall its existence or its passage.

Simcoe's statue outside Provincial Parliament Buildings

The British, who resumed trading amid the ruins and earned a bitter reputation among administrators and settlers for debauching the Indians with liquor, agreed to buy 500 acres (200 hectares) from the Mississauga tribe in 1787 for 1,700 pounds sterling worth of trade goods and food, including 24 brass kettles, 200 pounds of tobacco, 47 carrots, 10 dozen looking glasses, 24 laced hats, 2,000 gun flints, one bale of flowered flannel and,

naturally, this being the future site of Toronto, 96 gallons of rum.

The town of York, built and named with another bow to power overseas by John Graves Simcoe, the lieutenant-governor, was soon designated the capital of Upper Canada and almost as soon won a reputation for hard drinking. There were six taverns for a population of just over 400 and they were not held to modern hours, it seems, since landlords are on record as complaining they had to get up most nights to serve rum.

So widespread was York's

BACKGROUND

reputation for tippling, in fact, that a writer at the *Constellation,* a newspaper in Niagara, commented that the words 'We, the inhabitants of the Capital' should always be translated to read: 'We, the inhabitants of York, assembled at McDougall's over a glass of grog . . .'.

Fort York and the town were captured by US forces in the War of 1812, though the victory cost the invaders the life of explorer and brigade commander, General Zebulon Pike and a number of his soldiers when the powder magazine was blown up by the retreating British.

(During the US occupation the new parliament buildings were burned down with an unexpected but far-flung effect which you can see on any visit to Washington, DC. British troops attacking that city set fire to the president's residence in retaliation for the York blaze and to hide the scorch marks the building was painted with whitewash: hence the name White House, as it has been known ever since.)

However, the occupation lasted only a few days, then the US troops went home and the Town of York went on about its business. And it went right on growing. By March 6 1834, when it became the City of Toronto, it had a grand total of 9,254 residents and a fiery mayor, William Lyon Mackenzie, who felt so strongly about the need for responsible government that three years later he led an ill-planned and short-lived rebellion, based, naturally, in a

local tavern. Defeated, he fled to the US but returned to the city just 12 years later after a general amnesty, to run for the legislature — and win.

More, Mackenzie, who was the grandfather of William Lyon Mackenzie King, a Liberal prime minister of Canada earlier this century, was such a hero that in 1858, when he retired, public subscription bought him a home which is still standing, as a museum, at 82 Bond Street.

Responsible government came without rebellion and in 1867 independence came, too, also without rebellion, and the city kept growing, drawing immigrants mainly from Britain but with a trickle from the rest of Europe and, in the early years, a stream from south of the border, lured to Ontario by the abundance of land.

Nor had the French altogether disappeared from the scene with the loss of Fort Rouillé. There had always been French Canadian Torontonians since the days of St Jean Rousseau from Montreal, who had set up a trading post near the mouth of the Humber as early as 1780. It was he, in fact, who piloted the British schooner *Mississauga* bearing the new lieutenant-governor into the harbour where Simcoe was to build his capital. And the skipper of that Royal Navy ship was one Jean Baptiste Bouchette, certainly not from Limehouse or Yorkshire.

The Scots came in great numbers, fleeing the Highland Clearances, and the Irish, fleeing famine. By the early part of this century, in fact, the

So popular was rebel William Lyon Mackenzie that the people gave him a retirement home, now a museum

Toronto police force was mostly Irish — but in contrast to US cities these were Ulster Irish, Protestants all.

The make-up of the force has changed, of course, and so has the whole pattern of immigration and city settlement. Up until World War II Toronto was an Anglo-Saxon bastion but the post-war years brought a wave of Europeans, Dutch and Italian, Greek and German, Portuguese and Poles. And now new waves have rolled in, from the Caribbean and Latin America, from India and Pakistan, from Vietnam and Hong Kong, all forming part of the new fabric of the city.

On the positive side, for visitors, this has meant that the somewhat staid ways of the old Toronto are disappearing, that there are restaurants and entertainments of every kind representing cultures from around the world and that the population is far more varied and colourful than it was once upon a time.

But there are negatives, too, of which the visitor should be aware — trends to indicate Toronto is growing less law-abiding as it grows more diverse, with more reports of street gangs, drugs and violence. It is a long way from New York city yet. It is still a safe place, as it has been since Etienne Brulé hefted his canoe down the Humber, and you can still ride the subway in safety and walk the night-time streets. But now it can be seen that the little straggle of huts at the end of the portage is coming into the modern age.

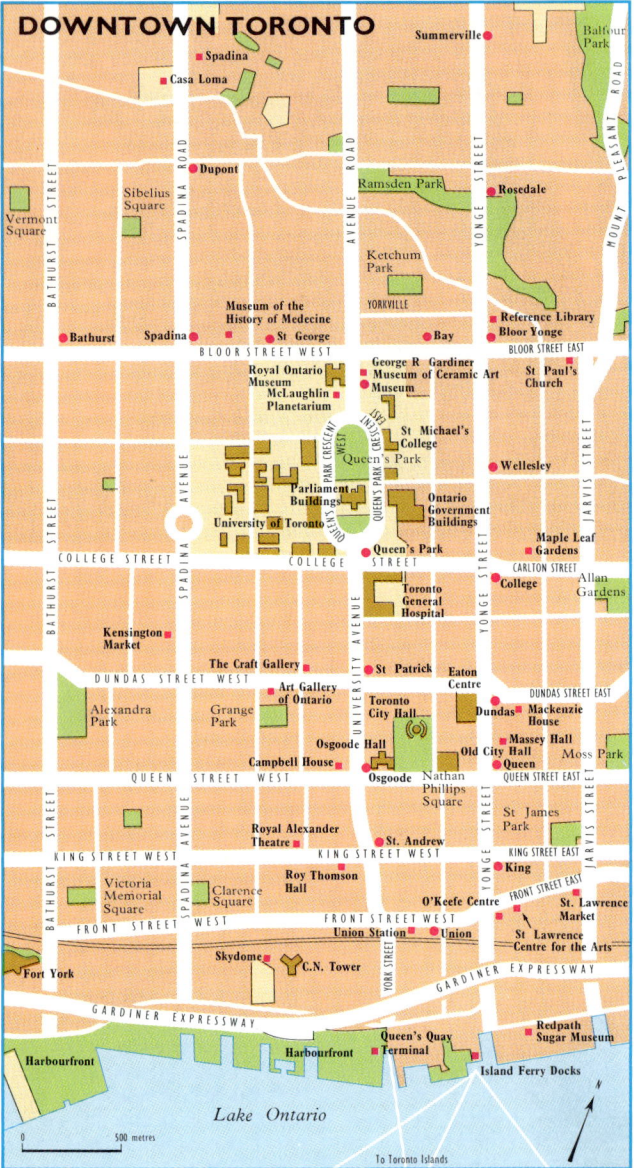

DOWNTOWN TORONTO

Summerville

Balfour Park

Spadina

Casa Loma

MOUNT PLEASANT ROAD

Dupont

SPADINA ROAD

AVENUE ROAD

YONGE STREET

Sibelius Square

Ramsden Park

Rosedale

Vermont Square

BATHURST STREET

Ketchum Park

YORKVILLE

Museum of the History of Medecine

Reference Library
Bloor Yonge

Bathurst   Spadina   St George   Bay

BLOOR STREET WEST

BLOOR STREET EAST

George R Gardiner Museum of Ceramic Art

St Paul's Church

Royal Ontario Museum
McLaughlin Planetarium

Museum

JARVIS STREET

St Michael's College

PARK CRESCENT EAST

QUEEN'S PARK CRESCENT WEST

Queen's Park

Wellesley

STREET

SPADINA AVENUE

Parliament Buildings

University of Toronto

Ontario Government Buildings

BATHURST

Queen's Park

Maple Leaf Gardens

COLLEGE STREET

COLLEGE   STREET

CARLTON STREET

College

Allan Gardens

YONGE STREET

Kensington Market

UNIVERSITY AVENUE

Toronto General Hospital

The Craft Gallery

St Patrick

Eaton Centre

DUNDAS STREET WEST

DUNDAS STREET EAST

Alexandra Park

Grange Park

Art Gallery of Ontario

Toronto City Hall

Dundas   Mackenzie House

Massey Hall

Osgoode Hall

Old City Hall

Moss Park

Campbell House

Queen

STREET

Osgoode   Nathan Phillips Square

QUEEN STREET EAST

QUEEN   STREET   WEST

STREET

AVENUE

St James Park

JARVIS STREET

Royal Alexander Theatre

St Andrew

YONGE STREET

KING STREET WEST

KING   STREET   WEST

KING STREET EAST

King

BATHURST

Victoria Memorial Square

SPADINA

Clarence Square

Roy Thomson Hall

FRONT STREET EAST

O'Keefe Centre

St Lawrence Market

FRONT   STREET   WEST

FRONT STREET WEST

Union Station   Union

St Lawrence Centre for the Arts

Fort York

Skydome

YORK STREET

C.N. Tower

GARDINER   EXPRESSWAY

GARDINER   EXPRESSWAY

Redpath Sugar Museum

Queen's Quay Terminal

Harbourfront

Harbourfront

Island Ferry Docks

0   500 metres

Lake Ontario

To Toronto Islands

WHAT TO SEE

Following John Graves Simcoe's
original plan, downtown Toronto
is laid out in a grid pattern
centred on Yonge Street, which
runs straight north from Lake
Ontario and forms the dividing
line for East and West street
designations. King Street East
runs in that direction from
Yonge, King Street West the
opposite way. In both cases the
numbers start at Yonge and
climb as you move away. North
and South streets are numbered
from the lakeshore.
Attractions in and around the
city can be reached by taxi,
limousine or rental car, of
course, but all can be visited by
public transport too, and
specific instructions on how to

*Looking out over downtown Toronto
from the CN Tower*

reach them by bus, streetcar or
subway can be obtained by
phoning the Toronto Transit
Commission (TTC) at 393-INFO.
(For more information, maps
and brochures call the Metro
Toronto Convention and Visitors
Association on 368-9821 or visit
its main kiosk in front of the
Eaton Centre at Yonge Street
and Dundas Avenue, where it
shares space with Five Star
Tickets. Other booths are
scattered about the Metro and
may be closer so telephone the
association for locations.)
The subway is fast, efficient,
graffiti-free and basically
simple. It runs in a giant narrow
U down Yonge Street from
Finch Avenue, through Union
Station, the hub of the system,
and north again under
University Avenue and Spadina
Avenue to Wilson Avenue. A
long cross-town Bloor Street

WHAT TO SEE

The Henry Moore Sculpture Centre in the Art Gallery of Ontario

Line runs from Kipling Avenue, in the west, under Bloor Street and Danforth Avenue to Kennedy Road in the east, with a surface spur running north and east to Scarborough Town Centre.

These lines all intersect with surface streetcar and bus routes and one ticket, with transfers, will take you through the whole Metro-wide system for a small cost. Exact change is required on streetcars and buses so it is wise to buy several tokens or tickets if you plan to make much use of the system.

Here are some of the places it can take you.

◆◆◆
ART GALLERY OF ONTARIO
317 Dundas Street West
British sculptor Henry Moore dominates this gallery even with its array of 12,000 works by artists ranging from Rembrandt to Picasso.

His is the first work you see as you approach the gallery and a huge new Henry Moore Sculpture Centre houses 131 bronzes and original plasters, 73 drawings and 689 prints, many of them donated by the artist after Toronto bought his bronze *The Archer* to grace its new city hall. Elsewhere, the Canadian Wing displays changing examples from the museum's huge collection of works by such artists as Emily Carr, David Milne, Homer Watson, Cornelius Krieghoff and the Group of Seven (see page 42). There are 20 galleries to feast upon and after that there is the Grange, behind the gallery and accessible from it, as a rich

dessert. The historic Georgian mansion, the oldest brick house in Toronto and the gallery's original home, has been restored as an elegant Canadian Gentleman's residence of the 1830s and is staffed by costumed and knowledgeable interpreters of pioneer life who go about the tasks of the day. Admission to the Grange is free with gallery admission.
Open: Tuesday to Sunday, Mondays from late May to Labour Day.
For information call 977-0414.

◆◆
BLACK CREEK PIONEER VILLAGE
Jane Street and Steeles Avenue
A whole mid-19th-century Ontario village, complete with human and animal inhabitants going about their daily lives. Watch the blacksmith, weaver and printer at their crafts, explore the grist mill, walk the boardwalks and the country roads. See, hear and smell what it was like to live in the rural Canada of Victoria's day. More than 30 buildings, including a general store, town hall, schoolhouse and hostelry are spread out around a pioneer farm and mill stream. Costumed villagers and farm folk add authenticity as they explain the troubles and joys of pioneer life. Buildings are closed 31 December to early March but visitors can take sleigh rides or go skating or cross-country skiing. Operating hours at other times vary by the season but the village is always open 10.00 to 16.00 daily, with opening time being extended to

18.00 on holidays and during July and August. About one hour by public transit from downtown, half that by car. (For information call 736-1733 or (a 24-hour tape) 661-6610).

Visitors to Black Creek Pioneer Village enjoy a taste of what life was like in Victorian days

◆◆◆
CANADA'S WONDERLAND
Maple, Ont
A lively 370 acre (150 hectare) theme park some 20 miles (30km) north of Toronto city hall featuring the Smurfs and Flintstones cartoon characters in Hanna Barbera Land, strolling musicians, water and thrill rides (and tame ones, too, for the small fry) and, at the Kingswood Music Theatre, big-name musicians and singers for adults. A major draw is the Salt Water Circus, featuring sealions and dolphins. There is plenty of noise and activity designed to keep you moving and spending, food is not cheap (and you are not allowed to bring a picnic)

Casa Loma has everything a dream castle should have

and the only places to sit in the shade are often the show pavilions, which can cost you again. But children love it. There are express GO buses from York Mills and Yorkdale subway stations (call 665-0022 for times and fares).

Open: Weekends during most of May and in the early autumn, daily in June, July and August, though hours vary. Admission package prices also vary widely in cost and coverage.

For details on hours and prices and for general information call 1-832-2205. For the Kingswood Theatre phone 1-832-8131.

◆◆◆
CASA LOMA
1 Austin Terrace
On a slight rise in the city's heart stands a 98-room castle built early in this century by millionaire royalist Sir Henry Pellatt, who spent a fortune on it, then found the taxes too high and turned it over to the community. Though it was three

years in the building and many more in the dreaming, he lived there for less than 10 years and never realised a major objective, to play host to members of the British royal family. Described by one critic as 'a mixture of 17th-century Scotch baronial and 20th-century Fox', Pellatt's castle, restored to its original grandeur, has everything a romantic would want: secret passageways, an 800ft (244m) underground tunnel, wine cellars, towers, stables, 30 bathrooms, 25 fireplaces, a palm room, a marble swimming pool, a kitchen range large enough to cook a whole ox, a shooting gallery and a bowling alley. You can explore it on your own and as you wander you can easily imagine Sir Henry and Lady Pellatt entertaining 3,000 guests at some grand ball, the tinkle of laughter in the great galleries,

the swish of silk, the shuddering
resonance of the mighty $75,000
pipe organ.
Open: every day except
Christmas, New Year's Day and
weekdays in January and
February. Hours are 10.00 to
16.00 except in July and August
when they are 09.30 to 16.00
There are frequent Murder
Mystery games played at the
castle, which offers a perfect
background.
For information on these and
other details telephone
923-1171.

♦♦♦
CN TOWER
301 Front Street West
The world's highest public
observation deck and a possible
sight of the spray from Niagara
Falls 30 miles (48km) away
across Lake Ontario are just two
of the attractions of this 1,815ft
(553m) tower, the world's tallest
free-standing structure. The Top
of Toronto revolving restaurant
at 1,150 feet (350m), reached by
an outside, glass-fronted
elevator (not for the faint of
heart) gives you a 360-degree
rotating view of the city, the
lake and miles of countryside
every 72 minutes. Or you can
dance at Sparkles Nightclub
high in the sky or shoot up
another 447 feet (136m) on an
inside elevator to the Space
Deck at 1,465 feet (447m) where
glass windows bank inward so
that you can look not only out
but down. Note that all this
requires a head for heights and
good visibility to make the trip
worthwhile so choose your day

Always on the skyline, the CN Tower

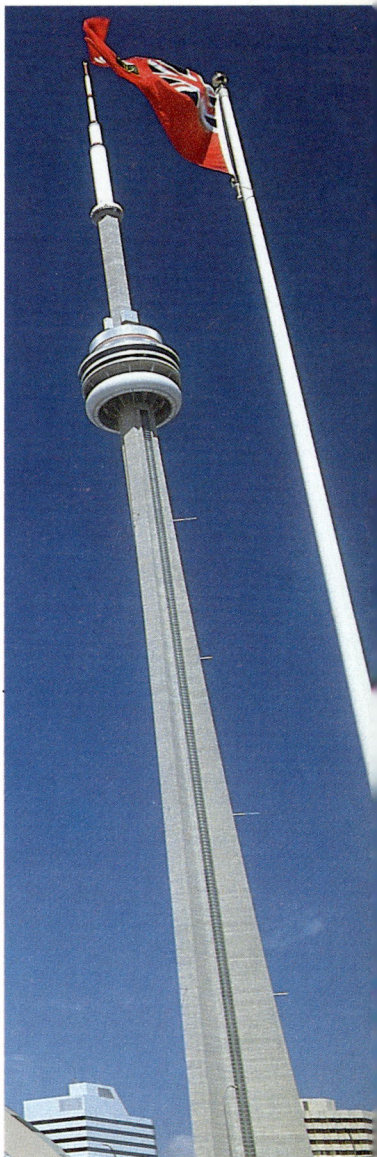

and your companion with care.
If high places are not for you,
consider going down instead of
up. Visit Tour of the Universe in
the basement beneath the tower
where the ride is only simulated
(see page 36).
Open: all year, Monday to
Friday, in winter, 10.00 to 22.00;
Saturday and Sunday, 09.30 to
23.00. In summer, Monday to
Sunday, 09.00 to midnight. To
find it, just look up. It can be
seen from anywhere along the
lakeshore and from many other
parts of Toronto.
For information call 360-8500.

◆
COLBORNE LODGE
South Entrance, High Park
Built in 1837 by artist/architect/
engineer John George Howard
and his wife, Jemima, and
superbly sited on a rise in High
Park overlooking Lake Ontario,
it is one of the oldest surviving
picturesque Regency villas in
North America. Howard
bequeathed the house and 165
acres (67 hectares) of grounds
to the city to form the nucleus of
Toronto's largest park (now 400
acres (162 hectares) thanks to
other donations), so that it sits
surrounded by nature, tall trees
and lush lawns, ponds and pools
and gardens. The house is
exceptional in the elegance of
its design but Howard was an
engineer, too, and it had its
practical side with a wine cellar,
summer and winter kitchens
and Toronto's first indoor
bathroom. Most of the original
furnishings are on display along
with Howard's watercolours of
early Toronto and there are
costumed guides to talk about

the lodge, the Howards and
John Howard's role in the
development of the city. Take a
picnic lunch to the park, use its
biking paths or playgrounds or
just its shady lawns and offer
yourself the lodge as a bonus.
Open: Monday to Saturday,
09.30 to 17.00; Sundays and
holidays, noon to 17.00.
Closed: Christmas Day, Boxing
Day (December 26), New Year's
Day and Easter Friday.
For information call 392-6916.

◆◆
FORT YORK
Garrison Road off Fleet Street
Built in 1793, blown up by the
retreating British during the
American invasion of April 1813,

*Military history is peacefully
re-enacted at Fort York, the scene
of a bloody battle in 1812*

rebuilt in 1816 and restored in
this century, the fort offers a
look at a national military past
that was a little more turbulent
than most visitors imagine.
Within the powder magazines,
blockhouses and barracks are
restored period rooms and
exhibits to tell that story and
there are uniformed guides to
enact and explain the
day-to-day military and social
life of the men and women who
lived there in colonial times. As
well, there are marches and
19th-century military drills to the
shrill of fifes and the beat of
drums. The fort was the
birthplace of Toronto and
perhaps deserves better than
being surrounded by traffic
arteries, as it is, but within its
fortified walls it is possible in
the traffic's lull to imagine
briefly those early days. And if
you wonder why it is not by the
water's edge as it once was, it is
not the fort that has been
moved, but the lake. Landfill has
shifted the shoreline south,
leaving the fort high and dry
north of Lakeshore Boulevard.
Open: Monday to Saturday,
09.30 to 17.00; Sunday, noon to
17.00, except from May to
September when Sunday hours
match those during the week.
For information call 392-6907.

◆◆◆
GEORGE R GARDINER
MUSEUM OF CERAMIC ART

111 Queen's Park, opposite the Royal Ontario Museum

The only museum of its kind in North America, this division of the Royal Ontario Museum is full of pottery treasures, 2,000 objects from high-heeled ceramic slippers to exquisite chocolate cups, mystical dragons, exotic perfume bottles and fragile flowered teapots. The Renaissance of Raphael and Michelangelo shines in the bold, bright colours of Italian majolica, English delftware recalls the reign of the Stuarts and Cromwell's Puritans and there are American pots dating back as far as 2000BC to tell of life in pre-Columbian days. As well, exhibits include more than 100 18th-century Meissen porcelain figures inspired by the Italian Commedia dell 'arte.

Open: Tuesday to Sunday, 10.00 to 17.00.

Closed: Mondays and national holidays. Admission to the ROM entitles you to tour the Gardiner. For information call 593-9300.

◆◆◆
HARBOURFRONT

Queen's Quay, York Street to Bathurst Street

The federal government acted as fairy godmother to turn this rundown waterside industrial strip on Queen's Quay into a

Harbourfront, a fun place for all

year-round people place for waterfront strolls and dances, concerts, lectures, sailing, musicals and entertainments, shopping and outdoor and indoor cafés. There's a walk that follows the water's edge and tables and benches for picnics, an antique market, craft works (pottery-making and such) and, if the budget allows, up-market shops in a magnificently renovated warehouse, Queen's Quay Terminal, which also houses the Premiere Dance Theatre. Stop at Queen's Quay Centre for a programme of events, which can range from ballet to ice canoe races. Some of Harbourfront's original appeal has been lost since it introduced apartment blocks to its lands but it is still a wonderful place to visit on a sunny afternoon and interesting any time. Do dress warmly in winter, though, when winds can be bitter even on a short walk near the water.
Open: every day but Christmas and New Year's Day, 10.00 to midnight.
Telephone 973-3000 for general information, 973-4000 for box office information.

◆
HOCKEY HALL OF FAME
Exhibition Place
This shrine of the unofficial national sport of Canada offers photographs, trophies, movies, artefacts, sticks, skates, goalie masks and histories of the game, the teams and the stars. But you have to be a fan or someone with real curiosity about the sport to get the most out of the exhibits. Canada's Sports Hall of Fame is in the

same building and offers a look at a broader range of activities.
Open: summer, 10.00 to 17.00 daily (during the Canadian National Exhibition open hours are extended to 20.00); winter, 10.00 to 16.30.
For information call 595-1345.

◆◆◆
MACKENZIE HOUSE
82 Bond Street
This is the home that his friends gave the fiery little rebel, William Lyon Mackenzie, in 1858 on his retirement from the provincial legislature. A printer, newspaper publisher and politician who fought with words and then with bullets for responsible government, he had led the disorganised anti-government forces in the Upper Canada Rebellion of 1837, then fled to the US when the revolt was quickly suppressed. But so popular were he and his cause that when he returned 10 years later he was re-elected to the provincial legislature where he served for another 10 years. (His daughter, born during the years of exile, was the mother of William Lyon Mackenzie King, Canada's prime minister during World War II.) Attached to the gas-lit Victorian townhouse is an exhibit gallery where his tempestuous story is told and a reconstructed 19th-century printing shop, complete with his hand-operated Washington flat-bed press and its original type. In the house itself costumed guides explain the family's lifestyle and demonstrate how domestic chores were carried out in the restored Victorian kitchen.

WHAT TO SEE

Summer visitors can go aboard this restored harbour tug, an exhibit at the Marine Museum

Afternoon tea is served.
Open: Monday to Saturday, 09.30 to 17.00; Sundays and holidays, noon to 17.00.
Closed: Christmas Day, Boxing Day (26 December), New Year's Day and Good Friday.
For information call 392-6915.

◆
MARINE MUSEUM OF UPPER CANADA
Exhibition Place
The stories of the fur trade and of Great Lakes warships and ferries are told here, along with the history of Toronto's harbour and a look at how the colonies used water transportation for fun and profit. There are superb ship models, too, and in summer, from May to October, visitors can swarm over a restored 1932 harbour tug named after the 1880 world sculling champion, Toronto's Ned Hanlan. There is a nice little restaurant (The Ship Inn) in the basement that is open for lunch only, and the building

itself is interesting. It served as the officers' quarters of Stanley Barracks, circa 1841, and was used as a quarantine station during World War I.
Open: Monday to Saturday, 09.30 to 17.00; Sundays and holidays, noon to 17.00.
Closed: Christmas Day and Boxing Day (26 December), New Year's Day and Good Friday.
For information call 392-6827.

◆◆
McLAUGHLIN PLANETARIUM
100 Queen's Park
You sink back in slothful comfort and the universe is yours, along with a laser-beam rock concert, if that is your desire, at this division of the Royal Ontario Museum. Under the 92ft (28m) dome 80 projectors and a superb sound system surround you with the starry gleam of the

night skies and images of distant planets, exploding stars, black holes and other phenomena. There's a three-dimensional model of the solar system and a 2,000-year-old sundial as well as computer games to illuminate the mysteries of the heavens. Shows change frequently. Children 6 to 15 must be accompanied by an adult, children under that age not admitted.
Open: Daily all year except for Christmas Day, New Year's Day and Mondays.
Call 586-5736 for information and show times.

◆◆◆
METRO TORONTO ZOO
Meadowvale Road, Scarborough
Some 710 acres (287 hectares) of woods, pastures and orchards have been transformed into African savannah, Malaysian rainforests, Western prairies and other habitats in this most modern and humane of zoos. The animals came first when the zoo was designed and they roam relatively freely over accurate re-creations of their home turf in outdoor reserves that mimic the terrains and even some artefacts (a Mayan temple, for example) of Africa, Australia, Eurasia, Indo-Malaya and the Americas. Meanwhile, in huge pavilions, climate control offers weather that is ideal for such diverse creatures as orangutans, kookaburras, beavers and alligators. There's a silent electric monorail train with air conditioning to take you where the deer and the antelope play, a Zoomobile for a longer

Tiger at the zoo, where animals roam freely (well, almost) in re-creations of their natural habitats

overview, four walking trails for the energetic (though some spots in the zoo are reachable only by train) and what was until recently the biggest McDonald's in the world to sustain you (though a picnic lunch would also fill the gap). Cross-country ski tours amid the animals are an unusual winter extra.
Open: every day but Christmas from 09.30, closing at 16.30 in winter, 19.00 in summer. Easiest to reach by rental or private car but accessible on public transit with a long bus ride.
For information call 392-5900.

◆
MONTGOMERY'S INN
4709 Dundas Street West at Islington Avenue
A handsome example of United Empire Loyalist or Late Georgian architecture, this 14-room inn has been restored

WHAT TO SEE

to its appearance during its heyday in the late 1840s when it was a centre of social life for the country around. Built in 1830 by Irish immigrant and militia captain Thomas Montgomery, it is not to be confused with the Yonge Street tavern of John Montgomery, which also flourished in the 1830s and was a meeting place for William Lyon Mackenzie's rebels of 1837. Costumed staff demonstrate the crafts and cooking methods of the time.
Open: Monday to Friday, 09.30 to 16.30; Saturday, Sundays and holidays, 13.00 to 17.00.
Closed: Christmas Eve and Christmas Day, New Year's Day and Good Friday.
For information call 394-8113.

◆◆◆
MUSEUM OF THE HISTORY OF MEDICINE
288 Bloor Street West
Everything from an Egyptian mummy to a Victorian baby's bottle can be found in the four small rooms of artefacts and exhibits that constitute Canada's major medical history museum. The mummy was autopsied in Toronto 14 years ago (no single cause of death was found) and is part of a display on that procedure. The bottle is part of the Drake paediatric collection of feeding objects, which dates from ancient times to 19th-century Europe. As well, there are scores of other exhibits illustrating 3,000 years of health care. Fascinating.
Open: Monday to Friday, 09.30 to 16.00. No admission charge for individuals.
For information call 922-0564.

◆◆◆
ONTARIO PLACE
955 Lakeshore Boulevard West at Exhibition Place
Built on and over the waters of Lake Ontario, this 96 acre (39 hectare) provincial government amusement park of steel and glass 'pods' looks like a set for a futuristic movie but offers very down-to-earth entertainment, everything from beer gardens and children's water games to a six-storey, wrap-around IMAX Cinesphere theatre, an open-air amphitheatre with big name entertainment (free with general admission) and a World War II destroyer, *HMCS Haida.* Can't be beaten on a warm summer afternoon or evening, whatever the entertainment. But take bathing suits for the children.
Open: mid-May to mid-September, Monday to Saturday, 10.00 to 01.00; Sunday 10.00 to 23.00.
For information call 965-7711.

◆◆◆
ONTARIO SCIENCE CENTRE
770 Don Mills Road at Eglinton Avenue East
A wonderland of hands-on science as entertaining as it is instructive. Touch, feel, manipulate, experiment, play. And learn the whole time. Among hundreds of other intriguing things, chat with a computer, guide a module to a landing on the moon, handle enough electricity to stand your hair on end (50,000 volts), hear a whisper, though not necessarily a romantic one, across a crowded room, run a television camera or appear on screen. Children are fascinated but so

With all its 'hands-on' exhibits, the Ontario Science Centre is one of Toronto's most fascinating and instructive attractions

are adults. The average visit lasts four hours, plus. Plan for at least that and use the map you are given on admission to make the best use of your time. Even then you may have to come back.

Open: every day but Christmas, 10.00 to 18.00, 21.00 on Fridays. Phone 429-0193 for information and extended summer hours.

Provincial Parliament Buildings, home of the Legislative Assembly, Romanesque and suitably imposing

◆◆◆
PROVINCIAL PARLIAMENT BUILDINGS

Queen's Park Crescent
Built to look governmental and imposing in the late 1800s, these pink sandstone and marble legislative buildings sit magisterially at the top of University Avenue in grassy, tree-shaded Queen's Park, a name that has become a synonym for the buildings themselves. The corridors and rooms are large and airy and the chamber on the second floor where the Legislative Assembly meets is appropriately formal. There are tours during business hours and visitors may attend sittings of the House (free tickets are necessary) when the 125-member assembly is in session (roughly October to December, February to June). The best time is usually the Question Period, from 14.00 to 15.00, when the opposition parties get a chance to attack the government on matters of current import.
For information call 965-4028.

◆◆◆
ROYAL ONTARIO MUSEUM

100 Queen's Park, Avenue Road and Bloor Street
One of the world's few major museums to combine art, science and archaeology, it is famous for its Ming tomb (the only one in the Western world), its general Chinese collection (the finest outside China) and its dinosaur skeletons, West Coast and Plains Indians displays and Egyptian relics, among many things. Visit the mastodon, stegosaurus and other giants in their prehistoric jungles, plumb the dark recesses of the Bat Cave, where special effects bring thousands of the little creatures to life, cringe from the

real and very lively tarantulas, scorpions and giant hissing cockroaches in the Life Sciences gallery, ponder the meaning of life in the new Gallery of Evolution — and amid the mummies of those who sought eternity so long ago on the banks of the Nile. One could spend a day or a week or a month among the fascinations in the main building without even glancing toward the three other nearby divisions of the museum (listed separately), the McLaughlin Planetarium, the Sigmund Samuel Building (Canadiana) and the George R Gardiner Museum of Ceramic Art.

Dinosaur skeletons in their prehistoric jungle setting at the Royal Ontario Museum

Open: year-round, 10.00 to 20.00 Tuesday and Thursdays; 10.00 to 18.00 the rest of the week.
For information call 586-5549.

◆◆
SIGMUND SAMUEL BUILDING
14 Queen's Park West
The scope and skill of Canada's pioneer craftsmen is on display at this haven for antique buffs and lovers of beauty. Period room settings, showcasing the finest in early Canadian silver, glass and woodenware, are a major attraction but so are the antique toys, weathervanes, farming implements, household tools and cooking utensils. On show, too, are paintings, pottery and sculpture by such artists as Cornelius Krieghoff, William Eby, Thomas Nesbitt and Louis Jobin and a magnificent set of

miniature models of pioneer
artefacts made early this
century by a craftsman born
before Confederation (1867). A
division of the Royal Ontario
Museum, the building is open
daily all year except for
Christmas Day and New Year's
Day.
Open: Monday to Saturday,
10.00 to 17.00; Sunday, 13.00 to
17.00. There is no admission
charge.
For information call 586-5549.

◆◆◆
SKYDOME
Base of the CN Tower
The newest attraction in the city,
this eight acre (3.25 hectare),
multi-million-dollar sports dome
in the heart of downtown
Toronto was opened in 1989. A
retractable roof 282 feet (86m)
above the playing field, high
enough to put a 31-storey
building underneath, rolls back
on sunny days to let baseball
and football fans and
concert-goers enjoy the
outdoors, rolls shut in stormy
weather. The figures are
staggering: it holds 52,000 for
baseball, 54,000 for football,
65,000 for concerts, has 24 fast
food outlets, including four
McDonald's (one of the largest
in North America), and contains
a 364-room hotel (with 70 rooms
overlooking the field), a health
club, a theatre, games booths
and a $13 million television
studio. As well, the giant central
video display board for replays
and messages, called, fittingly, a
Jumbotron, measures 115ft (35m)
by 33ft (10m). The Dome is the
new home of Toronto's major
league baseball team, the Blue

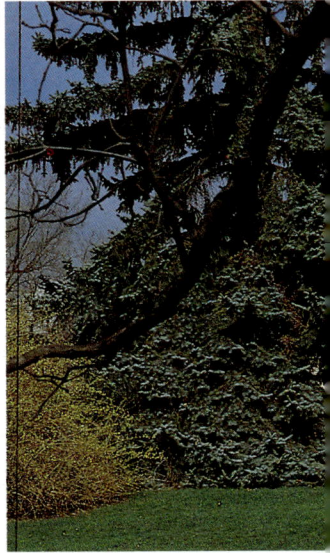

Jays, and the Toronto Argonauts
of the Canadian Football
League, but can be used for a
variety of sports, concerts and
exhibitions. Prices for games
and concerts will vary with the
event (check the local
newspapers for details) but
there are tours of the facility at
fixed prices.
For information call 341-3663.

◆
SPADINA
*285 Spadina Road beside Casa
Loma*
Complete with gaslight and
original furnishings, this 1866
mansion sits in six acres (2.5
hectares) of parkland and
garden and reflects the elegant
world of Toronto high society at
the turn of the century. Four
generations of the Austin family
lived in the home and the

Spadina House, whose furnishings reflect the life of four generations of the Austin family

furniture, art and decorations reflect the changing times, with Victorian, Edwardian and Art Nouveau influences. Guides introduce visitors to the upstairs/downstairs life of the Austins, their children and the domestic staff. The garden, one of Toronto's finest, offers more than 300 varieties of plants in an original setting. The house, incidentally, is pronounced 'Spa-DEE-na' though the street is pronounced 'Spa-DIE-na'.
Open: Monday to Saturday, 09.30 to 17.00; Sundays and holidays, noon to 17.00.
Closed: Christmas Day, Boxing Day (26 December), New Year's Day and Good Friday.
For information call 392-6910.

◆◆
TOMMY THOMPSON PARK
Leslie Street
A place for birdwatchers and nature lovers. This vast, and growing, landfill project once known as the Leslie Street Spit has become a paradise for birds and for people who want to escape the high-rise city except as a view across the bay. Ironically, it is that very city that keeps the three-mile (5km) spit growing now that harbour traffic has diminished and a breakwater is not as necessary. Rock and earth from the sites of the new skyscrapers still has to be put somewhere and the spit is the place. But it serves a good purpose since the park has become home to the largest gull population on the Great Lakes as well as a sanctuary for egrets, geese, ducks, herons, terns and

WHAT TO SEE

hundreds of smaller birds. Closed weekdays, the park can be reached at weekends by taking the Queen Street streetcar to Leslie Street and walking south or, on Sundays, by taking a bus from there that travels the length of the spit every 20 minutes. Other than that vehicle (and the trucks full of fill) admission is restricted to pedestrians and cyclists.

The striking architecture of the City Hall environs is reflected in the pool of Nathan Phillips Square

◆◆
TORONTO CITY HALL
100 Queen Street West at Bay Street
A marvel of modern architecture when completed after years of acrimony in 1965, the building, with twin towers cupping an oyster-shaped council chamber, is still eye-catching, though its efficiency as a workplace is somewhat less admired. Nathan Phillips Square, which fronts it, is home to sunbathers, demonstrators, rock concerts, brass bands, picnickers and people-watchers in summer and aglow with skaters on the frozen waters of the reflecting pool in winter. But whenever you go you will find British sculptor Henry Moore's monumental work *The Archer* there, weathering down the years. There are free tours weekdays, none on holidays.
For information call 392-7341.

◆◆◆
TORONTO ISLANDS
across the harbour
Another waterfront attraction that may just be the best because so much of it was contributed by nature, not man. The six islands, which stretch in an arc across the waterfront to form the harbour, are reached on Metro Parks Department ferries which leave from a dock south of the Westin Harbour Castle Hotel at the end of Yonge Street (but note that the dock is reached via walkways at the west side of the hotel, near the end of Bay Street). Avoid the trip on summer weekends when the islands are thick with people; but on weekdays they offer cool breezes and a bucolic retreat for lazing, sunning and picnicking. There are beaches and swimming but the lake water is cool to the uninitiated and sometimes polluted (signs will warn visitors if it is). Shady

The Toronto Islands make a cool retreat across the harbour, with plenty of activities on offer

lagoons and canals wind hither and yon and at Centre Island you can rent paddleboats and canoes to explore their lengths (if you can avoid the former, the latter can be a wonderful way to drift away a sleepy afternoon). Or you can rent a bicycle for a leisurely tour of the parkland. Food is available and there is a small, 14 acre (5.5 hectare) amusement area called Centreville, which is modelled on a turn-of-the-century village. Admission is free and it has 15 rides, games, arcades, miniature golf and a small petting farm for children. In winter the ferry service is less frequent but available for cross-country skiers or well-bundled walkers. Ferry fares are minimal but changeable.
Telephone the Parks Department on 392-8193 for times and fares.

◆◆
TOUR OF THE UNIVERSE
Base of the CN Tower
A trip to the year 2019 and a spaceship flight to Jupiter played absolutely straight, with a 3-D boarding pass, check-points, customs, immigration and health controls, inoculations (by painless — and harmless — light beams), seat belts and a 70mm-wide-screen simulation of flight that can have you gripping the arm-rest. Rated among the top 10 rides in North America (though it is not technically a ride), it is all superbly done with the finishing touch being the deadly serious way it is all handled. You may think it is a game but they play it for real, which adds greatly to the effect. Journeys last approximately one hour.
Open: all year, with summer hours 10.00 to 22.00 and winter hours varying. Earthlings 12 years of age or under must be over three feet (one metre) tall to make the voyage.
For information call 363-TOUR.

Excursions from Toronto

There are multitudes of day trips and weekend jaunts one can make out of Toronto, to Old Fort Henry at Kingston or the beaches or ski slopes of Georgian Bay, to a hundred villages or beauty spots for such things as fall fairs, maple sugar or autumn colour. The city sits just south of a vast cottage country and just north of the US border, so there are attractions in every direction. But four top the list by a considerable margin, one for its sheer magnificence and power, one for its period charm and the other two for their artistry.

♦♦♦
NIAGARA FALLS

Just 90 miles (145km) away around Lake Ontario, one of the natural wonders of the world thunders away the years carrying 34.5 million gallons (157 million litres) of water a minute over Canada's Horseshoe Falls in an awesome display of raw power. It is the major falls at the site, 177ft (54m) high and carrying 90 per cent of the water (the others are Rainbow Falls on the US side of the border and Bridal Veil Falls), and it is magnificent, no matter the viewpoint or the season. You can look down at it from towers, go behind its downfall, approach it from below in what seems a very tiny boat or simply stand by the brink mesmerised by the sight and the sound. If the weather is pleasant get some idea of the scale first by taking a walk of just under a mile (1.5km) along the brink of the gorge from

The American Rainbow Falls thunder into the Niagara River

WHAT TO SEE

Kleinburg

MAJOR MACKENZIE

Kortright Centre

Canada's
Wonderland

MAPLE

50

VAUGHAN

400

Richvale

11

27

WOODBRIDGE

7

Concorde

West Don River

East Don River

7

Claireville
Conservation Park

YONGE STREET

STEELES AVENUE WEST

Rowntree
Mills Park

Black Creek
Pioneer Village

York University

Sunshine Beach
Waterpark

Funstation

NORTH YORK

FINCH AVENU

Gibson House

400

Downsview
Airport

The Puppet Centre

427

401

Pearson
International
Airport

Humber River

Joseph D Carrier
Art Gallery

AVENUE ROAD

Eglington
Flats

ETOBICOKE

EGLINGTON AVENUE WEST

11

Glen Agar
Park

ISLINGTON AVENUE

YORK

11A

Centennial
Park

DUNDAS STREET

YONGE STREET

427

Montgomery's Inn

5

BLOOR STREET

High Park

Spadina
Casa Loma

Royal Ontario
Museum

Queen's
Park

5

Colborne Lodge

TORONTO

Enoch
Turner
Schoolhou

Sunnyside
Beach

Canada Sports
Hall of Fame

CN Tower

Ontario Place

Marine Museum

Harbourfront
Park

LAKESHORE BOULEVARD

Humber Bay

Toronto Island
Airport

Centreville

2

Toronto Islands

TORONTO AREA

404

17th AVENUE

RICHMOND
HILL

MARKHAM

Green
River

7

East Rouge River

Rouge River

48

STEELES AVENUE EAST

404

Finch East
Park

SCARBOROUGH

Metropolitan
Toronto Zoo

Glen Rouge
Park

VICTORIA PARK AVENUE

401

Scarborough
Civic Centre

Edward's
Gardens

Thomson
Memorial Park

Morningside
Park

Sunnybrook
Park

Ontario
Science Centre

EAST YORK

EGLINTON AVENUE EAST

East Point
Park

2

Taylor Creek
Park

KINGSTON ROAD

Todmorden Mills
Museum

5

Bluffers Park
Scarborough Bluffs

N

Lake   Ontario

Tommy Thompson
Park

0   5 km

0   3 miles

Rainbow Bridge to Table Rock, then gain entrance to the tunnels behind the falls through Table Rock House. For a small fee you are fitted out with raincoat and boots and take an elevator down 125 feet (38m) to the first tunnel, which offers you three different views of the incredible wall of water. And wall is the word. Curtain has too frail a connotation to describe that mighty, battering, deafening downpour. After that, get another close-up view of the falls aboard the *Maid of the Mist*, which you will find at the end of a well-signed trail down the gorge. Again you pay a small fee and don raincoat and boots but this time you see the downfall from the front, bobbing about like a frail cork on the surging waters (it operates from mid-May to late October).

Views from the look-out towers are scenic enough but they do not give you the vision of brute power you get, deafened and drenched, at the base of the falls. The towers are a better bet at night when the falls are illuminated (approximately 21.00 to midnight in summer, 19.00 to 22.00 in winter). In addition, in winter, when ice formations and frozen spray can create a fairyland effect, citizens join the Niagara Parks Commission, hotels and businesses in creating a Christmas-time effect with thousands of coloured

Horseshoe Falls illuminated: the best time to view Niagara Falls from a tower is at night

◆◆◆
NIAGARA-ON-THE-LAKE

Best known these days as the home of the world's only annual Shaw Festival, this little town of some 13,000 on the shores of Lake Ontario was once (1791-1796) the capital of Upper Canada. It lost that title — and the legislature — to the upstart Fort York because, authorities said, it was too close to the US border. And, for once, authorities were right. In 1813 the Americans came in and burned the place to the ground. However, the gracious 19th-century homes that arose from the ashes of Newark, as it was then called, are with us yet and lend the town its special appeal. It is small enough to explore on foot and one of the joys of a visit is a stroll through the old section and along Queen Street. There one finds gift and antique shops, tea rooms and ice cream parlours, all with a carefully studied old-fashioned air, which comes to its fullest flower in the Niagara Apothecary Museum with its graceful 1866 bottles and beautifully labelled 19th-century jars. An ideal plan is to arrive early for the theatre and spend some time strolling through the town, then enjoy a picnic by the water or a dinner at one of the local hostelries. Accommodation tends to have an old-fashioned air, as well, with Bed & Breakfast establishments and several inns doing a roaring business in the summer theatrical season. The festival,

bulbs in a three-month (mid-November to mid-February) Festival of Lights. The town of Niagara Falls itself is very commercial but the falls, on Niagara Parks Commission land, make up for any gaudiness. The Parks Commission, incidentally, owns land right along the 35-mile (56km) length of border and its gardens are famous. They are well worth a drive, say while on the way from Niagara Falls to Niagara-on-the-Lake. The falls can be reached from Toronto by car on the Queen Elizabeth Way as well as by bus, special coach tours (call Gray Coach Lines on 393-7911) and by train (call VIA rail on 366-8411).

which began as a low-key tribute to Shaw in 1962, now presents a full May-to-October season devoted to the witty iconoclast and his contemporaries, with no less than three theatres on the go. For tourist information call 1-468-4263 (there's a charge from Toronto) and for festival information call 361-1544 (toll free) from Toronto. Niagara-on-the-Lake is 80 miles (130km) from Toronto and can be reached by car using the Queen Elizabeth Way or by Gray Coach.

◆◆◆
STRATFORD

Stratford as the home of William Shakespeare is a familiar concept, and in this little community 98 miles (157km) west of Toronto that tie is perpetuated, even though the original Stratford-upon-Avon lies several thousand miles to the east. More than 150 years ago citizens of what was then a tiny hamlet renamed the Little Thames River the Avon and set about cultivating a relationship with the Bard based on nothing more than a name. But in 1953, when the Stratford Festival was born with Alec Guinness play-ing Richard III upon a makeshift stage under a tent, the link was completed. Today Stratford offers one of the world's great cultural experiences, presenting not just Shakespeare and other works in the Festival Theatre but every form of theatre and music, ranging from folk songs to opera in the Avon Theatre and Third Stage and in privately owned theatres. It attracts stars from around the globe and

patrons from as far. There are 172 acres (70 hectares) of parkland along the Avon and 19th-century public buildings and homes to admire and, best of all, there is a sense of peace, a calm, unhurried pace that fits in well with Shakespeare. The season is May through October. Tourist information can be obtained from the Stratford Visitors bureau on (519) 271-5140 (long distance from Toronto) and festival information by calling a Toronto number, 373-4471. Stratford can be reached by car from Toronto using Highway 401 west or by train (VIA Rail) or bus (Gray Coach Lines).

◆◆◆
McMICHAEL CANADIAN COLLECTION
Kleinburg

The Group of Seven, formed by that number of artists back in 1920, captured Canada on canvas with a realism that caught the eyes of the world. This is one of the great collections of the group's work, but alongside it there is also an important collection of works by other Canadians such as Emily Carr and Clarence Cagnon and Indian and Inuit art and sculpture. The whole is magni-ficent and the setting, over-looking the beautiful Humber River valley, is unbeatable. *Open:* 1 May to 31 October, daily 10.00 to 17.00; 1 November to 30 April, Tuesday to Sunday, 11.30 to 16.30. About an hour north of Toronto by car using Highway 400.
For information call 1-893-1121.

PEACE AND QUIET

Wildlife and Countryside in and around Toronto

Toronto lies on the shores of Lake Ontario and within easy reach of extensive areas of forest in southern Ontario. This makes it an ideal centre for visitors who appreciate scenery and natural history, the lake itself attracting wildfowl, waders and gulls in large numbers and woodlands harbouring varied mammals, birds and plants. The further away from Toronto you travel, the more natural is the landscape. Many of the forests further north are relatively unspoilt and even the wildlife around the city itself is representative of the region as a whole. Insects of all shapes and sizes abound in the forests and woodland birds such as woodpeckers, warblers, hawks and flycatchers are numerous. Large mammals are also often seen: deer, moose and bear are common and in Algonquin Provincial Park are especially confiding.

Gentle Giant. Although formidable to look at, the moose is actually a shy vegetarian

PEACE AND QUIET

From a botanical point of view, the forest floors are a delight, being rich in mosses, ferns and orchids. For a few days in the autumn, the burnished leaves are a memorable sight and when they fall they create a patchwork of shades which vie, in terms of colour, with fungi of all shapes and sizes.

Toronto and Lake Ontario

Stretching south from the waterfront of Toronto, Lake Ontario disappears into the distance like a huge, inland sea and, to add to the maritime effect, many of the birds that it harbours would be equally at home on the eastern seaboard of North America. Terns and gulls breed on some of the remote headlands and islands while in winter, vast numbers of waterbirds dot the surface of its waters.

Harbours and beaches play host to mixed flocks of herring gulls and ring-billed gulls, the former being the more numerous of the two. Although superficially similar, ring-billed gulls can be identified by their slightly smaller size, the pale eye with a dark 'eye-brow' and the 'ringed' bill. From autumn to spring, a variety of more unusual species sometimes joins these flocks and careful scrutiny sometimes reveals glaucous, Iceland, Franklin's or Bonaparte's gulls in among the larger birds.

Autumn and winter are the seasons for the wildfowl which congregate around the shores of the lake and tens of thousands of birds are often recorded in a season. From the Toronto Islands and lake-shores to the

east of the city, vast rafts of birds can be seen. Numbers are often under-estimated since bobbing and diving birds are difficult to count and it is often only when flocks take to the wing that a true idea of the numbers involved can be obtained. Canada geese mingle with scaup, bufflehead and long-tailed ducks, and many other species are also seen during spring and autumn migration. By late winter, most of the male ducks have acquired their breeding plumage and often display to each other in separate-species flocks. In among the ducks, double-crested cormorants sometimes swim and dive for fish and lucky observers may see great northern divers (common loons) resplendent in their black and white summer plumage.

Named for their native homeland –
Canada geese and goslings

In most years, the level of Lake
Ontario drops slightly by late
summer and even a slight drop
exposes beaches along its
shoreline. These are much
favoured by migrant waders
which pass through in vast
numbers from late July to
October. Semi-palmated
sandpipers, dunlin, lesser
yellowlegs and least sandpipers
are all abundant in suitable
habitats and identifying them
can prove a stimulating
challenge.

Marshes and Pools
Wetland habitats abound in
southern Ontario and provide an
endless source of fascination for
anyone with an interest in
natural history. Birds and
mammals patrol the pool
margins and open water, many
species feeding on fish and
amphibians. These in turn prey
upon aquatic larvae of the biting
insects that can make the
visitor's life a misery during the
summer months.
Open marshes with sedges and
rushes are found beside river
courses and much of the forest
is also decidedly wet underfoot.
Alder woodland, in particular, is
often swampy and pools of open
water are not uncommon, thus
providing ideal habitats for
American toads and gray
treefrogs, which spend much of
their lives on land but have to
return to the water to spawn.
Whether in water or land, the
marshes' smaller inhabitants
have to be constantly vigilant
since green herons, great blue
herons and American bitterns
are ever alert for a meal. The
latter species, with its mottled

and streaked brown plumage, shows remarkable camouflage as it creeps stealthily through the vegetation. The instant that it spots a meal, however, this apparent lethargy disappears and a lightning strike secures the victim.

American woodcock and sora rails skulk around the margins of ponds and lakes, which are often fringed with reed-mace (cat-tail), searching the muddy margins for insects, snails and other invertebrates. Blue-winged teal and that most elegant of wildfowl, the wood duck, keep close to cover while, in the open water, pied-billed grebes swim and dive and belted kingfishers and ospreys plunge from overhead perches. There are also mammals to be seen in these marshy habitats and conical heaps of vegetation built in the shallows are a sure sign of the presence of muskrats, endearing rodents which build their homes out of reach of land predators. They are often seen swimming across the water to reach them and can be identified by their long, naked tails which are laterally flattened. The muskrat's diet is largely plant material but by contrast mink are strictly carnivorous. Rather shy animals, they are competent swimmers and somewhat similar to, although smaller than, the river otters with which they coexist.

Algonquin Provincial Park
Lying less than 220 miles (350km) north of Toronto, Algonquin Provincial Park is a vast area of Canadian wilderness. Its 3,000 square miles (7,700 sq km) comprise lakes, rivers, marshes, rocky outcrops and extensive forests containing both deciduous and coniferous tree species. The wide variety of Algonquin's trees is due to its position at the geographical divide between the coniferous forests, which dominate northern Canada, and the mixed woodlands of the Great Lakes region. This diversity has encouraged a wonderful range of other plants and animals to the park, many of which are more characteristic of sub-arctic environments.

Despite its great size, Algonquin is still accessible to both the casual visitor and the intrepid

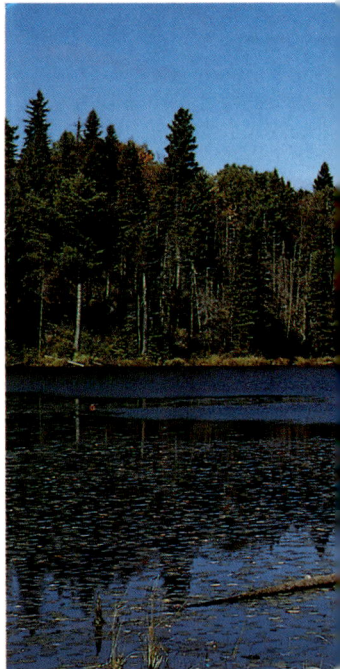

explorer. Between Huntsville and Whitney, Highway 60 traverses the southern tip of the park and from here and the forest tracks and side roads, there is plenty to be seen. Well-informed rangers at the Park Museum will advise you on the best spots on a day-to-day basis and should also be consulted if you wish to venture further into the wilderness. Facilitating this, a network of hiking trails and over 620 miles (1,000km) of canoe routes allow further exploration and

Some of Canada's finest wilderness areas are to be found within Algonquin Provincial Park

designated campgrounds and lodges afford overnight stays. Around the margins of lakes on which great northern divers (common loons) and ospreys fish, grow woodlands of maple, birch, cherry, balsam and spruce. Warblers and red-eyed vireos forage among the foliage for insects, while in moss-covered glades and clearings, orchids, and plants of Labrador tea and leather-leaf grow in profusion. Algonquin is perhaps most famous for the variety and the often confiding nature of its mammals. Beaver, white-tailed deer, moose, black bear and red fox are common and

frequently seen, but it is the park's timber wolves which are most renowned. During the late summer and autumn, their howls are a familiar sound as family parties gather together before the onset of winter. Visitors have little to fear from these impressive predators because, despite their reputation, much of their diet is fruit, carrion and small mammals and birds. It is only in the dead of winter that large packs form to hunt down quarry as large as deer or moose.

The Wildlife of Algonquin Provincial Park

Although the short-term visitor to Algonquin cannot fail to be impressed by its scenery and wildlife, a longer stay will yield a far greater variety of plants and animals. By exploring the forest trails at length, the visitor will come across more retiring creatures and have time to observe some of their more intriguing activities.

The signs and handiwork of beavers are conspicuous throughout the park. These industrious rodents, which may weigh as much as 55lbs (25kg), build dams which flood considerable areas of woodland and, surrounded by water, the beavers construct their 'lodge'. Built of twigs and mud, their home is only accessible from beneath the water's surface, making it invulnerable to attack from many predators. Bark and twigs of aspen, birch and maple are their favourite food and they sometimes fell whole trees to serve as a winter larder. Larger lakes are often grazed

Beavers will sometimes fell a whole tree for winter food

by moose. These huge beasts, males of which have immense sets of antlers for most of the year, are especially fond of plants growing under the water's surface. Moose have long legs and can swim extremely well, so that during the height of summer, when biting insects are at their most troublesome, they spend much of the day almost completely submerged. Sometimes the only sign of their presence is a nose, ears and antlers. Many of Algonquin's other inhabitants are more inconspicuous but, fortunately, most of the birds can be located by their calls or songs, which to the trained ear are readily distinguishable. Some of the forest dwellers, however, do not give any clues as to their whereabouts and must be located by persistent observation or luck.

The spruce grouse is just such a creature: neither shy nor afraid of man, this remarkable bird knows exactly where to sit in the undergrowth to get the best effect from its mottled plumage. In dappled light it is almost invisible among the tangle of fallen leaves and twigs and to enhance its camouflage, it also shows great reluctance to move. Once it has been found the bird allows a close approach and to be able to sit quietly and watch a spruce grouse close-to is a memorable experience.

The Forests of Ontario

Canada is renowned for its forests and despite the activities of large-scale commercial

foresters, much of the country is still cloaked by trees. Even within the boundaries of Toronto, Morningside Park and James Gardens hold interesting, semi-natural woodland and within a short distance of the city, fascinating tracts of forest can still be found harbouring a wealth of plant and animal life. The forests of Ontario are strikingly different according to their position within the state. Those immediately around Toronto are largely a mixture of deciduous trees (those whose leaves fall in the autumn) with a smaller proportion of conifers, which generally retain their leaves throughout the year. However, as you travel north in the state, the proportions change and conifers predominate with black spruce, white spruce, larch and jack pine being among the commonest species.

The reason for this change in forest type is the latitude and climate of the land past and present. At the time of the last Ice Age, much of Canada lay under a blanket of ice which excluded vegetation almost completely, but as the ice retreated northwards, hardy plants began to colonise this new landscape of pools and marshes. The first to do so were the larches, spruces and birches which now comprise the boreal forests, but as the climate warmed up further south these species were replaced by the less hardy trees such as maple, red oak and oak which reach the northern limit of their ranges.

The air is often filled with the

scent of pines, and as a testament to its clarity, lichens, which are especially sensitive to pollution, festoon the trees. Red squirrels chatter noisily and scamper among the branches, pausing to nibble the seeds from fir cones, their dexterous hands assisting them greatly in this process.

Black bears forage on the ground for berries, fruits and small mammals, while in the foliage above, warblers and flycatchers forage for insects among the lichens and leaves. Woodpeckers, such as the northern flicker, bore holes in the trunks and branches in search of wood-boring insect larvae, especially where the tree is dead. On the other hand,

the delightfully named yellow-bellied sapsucker often drills into living wood, causing the sap to run.

Forest Life
The forests bordering the Great Lakes contain a rich variety of trees and the leaves of the deciduous species which predominate produce stunning colours for a few autumn days prior to their being shed. During the spring and summer, the woods are full of new life, but the falling leaves forecast the onset of winter when food is most difficult to come by and survival is the name of the

A chipmunk searching for insect food in tree bark

game.
The wildlife of the woodland has adapted to these seasonal changes in a variety of ways. For example, although some birds can endure the harsh winters, many migrate south to more temperate regions. Most reptiles, amphibians and insects survive in a state of dormancy and mammals, too, have had to adapt in order to survive the hardships of the biting Canadian winters.

White-tailed deer have little option but to persevere until the ice and snow relinquish their grip on the land, their thicker winter coats giving them added insulation. Beavers, on the other hand, retreat to their snug lodges around which they have already built up a large supply of winter rations. Other mammals, such as the charming eastern chipmunk, build up their own fat reserves and hibernate through the worst of the weather. Come the spring, with its promise of bountiful food supplies, the chipmunks soon wake up and make up for lost time and energy reserves.

April and May sees the arrival of returning migrant birds whose songs add to those of the resident species. Each songster is advertising his presence within a territory and trying to lure a mate. If successful, a nest is built with different species occupying sites from the forest floor to the tree canopy.

By May and June, plant life burgeons in the woods and this encourages a wide range of herbivorous insects such as caterpillars. The fate of many of these is to feed the hungry mouths of young birds, but enough survive to give rise to colourful butterflies such as spice-bush swallowtails, mourning cloaks, fritillaries and skippers.

Moths are also abundant but hide by day among fallen leaves or on tree bark. After dark, they are often attracted to car headlights or outside lamps, and many species, such as hawk moths, are surprisingly large. These too are preyed upon and form the diet of a variety of nocturnal animals such as bats and the common nighthawk.

Toronto's Warblers
During the harsh Canadian winters, the forests of southern Ontario, although stately in their mantle of snow and ice, are comparatively silent: those creatures that have not hibernated or moved south for the winter are quietly and busily engaged in the search for food. Come the spring, however, the woods come alive with bird song and this joyful sound helps rejuvenate the life of the forest. Many of the songsters are warblers, of which at least ten species regularly breed within a short distance of Toronto. A further 10 species breed more locally in Ontario and several more, such as Cape May warbler, palm warbler and Nashville warbler, pass through on passage. In fact, on a good day during spring migration, it is quite possible to see more than half the number of species which breed in the whole of North America, and on top of this there will be vireos and flycatchers to look at.

This yellow warbler is one of at least 20 species of warbler that might be seen around Toronto

Some warblers, such as the yellow warbler, black-and-white warbler and chestnut-sided warbler, prefer the deciduous woodlands which border the Great Lakes, while other species, like the Canada warbler and Blackburnian warbler, haunt the coniferous woodlands so typical of northern Canada. Since Algonquin Provincial Park harbours a good mixture of both forest types, it is a particularly rewarding spot to search. Some of the species found here have somewhat misleading names: despite their titles, ovenbirds, which resemble miniature thrushes, and American redstarts both belong to the family of North American wood warblers. Spring is a particularly rewarding time of year to look for warblers because the males of most species will be singing and even migrant birds on passage join in the chorus.

Although by July and August, most birds will have finished breeding and, therefore, singing too, the numbers of birds make up for this because both adult and juvenile birds will be present.

By late summer, identifying them can prove a real challenge because of the variation in plumages. In many species, males have a different plumage from females, summer plumage is different from winter and juveniles are different from adults. The end result is that, at this time of year, no two birds ever seem to look exactly alike!

Farmland and Open Country
Toronto and the surrounding countryside of Ontario has been occupied by Man for centuries and during this time he has had

a profound influence upon the environment. The most noticeable effect has been the clearance, in many areas, of the trees which once cloaked the region. Much of this land has been, and still is, used for agriculture, but where the fields have been allowed to revert to the wild, an interesting selection of wildlife can be found and the open terrain makes observation all the more easy.

In drier areas, milkweed plants with their umbels of pink flowers are quick to colonise, the leaves becoming food in the summer months for the brightly coloured and poisonous caterpillars of monarch

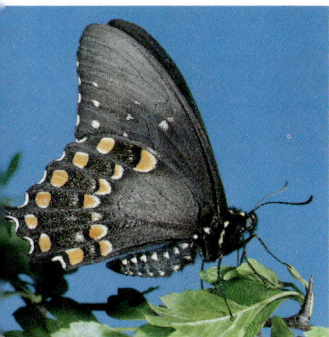

Spice-bush swallowtail

butterflies. Skipper and swallowtail butterflies also visit flowers to feed on the nectar, and grasshoppers and bush crickets hop among the low vegetation, many falling victim to vigilant eastern kingbirds or ground-hunting eastern garter snakes.

After dark, moths take to the wing, many being consumed by common nighthawks, birds with large eyes and gaping mouths which catch insects on the wing. They nest in a simple scrape on the ground where their cryptic plumage renders them almost invisible as they sit motionless throughout the day. Also nesting on the ground are killdeer, elegant plovers whose name derives from their loud alarm call. Their two black breast bands and conspicuous chestnut rump in flight make them easy to identify.

Overhead, American kestrels and red-tailed hawks patrol the skies scanning the ground for small mammals and birds which scurry into the cover of long grass and low shrubs in which horned larks build their nests. Strikingly marked bobolinks and eastern meadowlarks use low bushes as convenient perches. The latter species also uses these lookouts as song perches, while bobolinks sing in flight over their territory.

By the late summer and autumn, flowers and bushes have started to produce their seeds and fruits, and red berries attract the attentions of ravenous cedar waxwings, unmistakable with their subtle pink plumage and conspicuous crests. Prior to migration, large flocks of red-winged blackbirds and brown-headed cowbirds wheel through the skies, descending like a cloud to the ground to feed.

Buffalo and Niagara
The Niagara Falls are among the most spectacular and widely visited natural wonders of the world and few people can fail to

be impressed by their splendour. However, while visiting this world famous beauty spot, the keen observer can also see a wide variety of waterbirds on the Niagara River, many of which may even be seen from the *Maid in the Mist* boat which travels to the foot of the falls.

The attraction of the Niagara River to the birds that frequent its waters lies partly in its position between Lakes Ontario and Erie and partly in the fact that it seldom freezes over. In addition, migrant landbirds pass through the Niagara peninsula in spring and autumn and add further variety to an already exciting species list.

From the road which runs parallel with the river, huge flocks of gulls can be seen. At all seasons, herring and ring-billed gulls predominate, but at any time of year, apart from the height of summer, small numbers of up to 10 other species may be seen. Glaucous and Iceland gulls are comparatively large, white-winged birds and therefore easy to pick out in flight, whereas kittiwakes, Franklin's, Bonaparte's and black-headed gulls stand out because of their smaller size.

On the waters of the river, small numbers of divers and grebes mix with often sizeable flocks of ducks. As on Lake Ontario itself, bufflehead, goldeneye and canvasback are common with many other species occurring in smaller numbers. Long-tailed ducks, often known as 'oldsquaws' on account of their cackling calls, can also be numerous. The drakes have long tail-plumes from which they gain their name and these show up especially well in flight. Like the shores of Lake Ontario to the east of Toronto, those of Lake Erie to the west of Buffalo are excellent for migrant waders, generally referred to as shorebirds in American books. During April and May, and from July to October, more than a dozen species can be seen in a single day. Short-billed dowitchers, dunlin, pectoral sandpipers, turnstone and semi-palmated sandpipers abound, the numbers of adult birds being supplemented in autumn by juvenile birds in smart, fresh plumage.

Migration

Toronto's climate is one of extremes: the summers are hot, but in winter the grip of ice and snow can be unremitting. Some animals can tolerate these extremes while others avoid the winter by hibernating or migrating south before the weather changes for the worse. Many of Toronto's passerine birds feed on insects and consequently have to move south in winter in order to feed. Some species move relatively short distances in response to prevailing weather conditions, but others make predictable and annual long-distance migrations covering thousands of miles. Broad-winged hawks and barn swallows are among those which undertake journeys which may take them as far south as Central and South America. While migrating, these birds often become concentrated in

The drake's tail feathers make the long-tailed duck unmistakable at all times of the year

certain areas, and although nowhere around Toronto can compare with Point Pelee in western Ontario, the shores of Lake Ontario and Long Point, 125 miles (200km) southwest on the shores of Lake Erie, still yield impressive numbers of birds in spring and autumn. In the winter, these same areas can also be good for visitors from the arctic because, surprising as it may seem, to them Toronto's winters are comparatively mild. Glaucous and Iceland gulls are regular and there is a good chance of seeing snowy owls and rough-legged buzzards as well. Migration in the animal kingdom is not entirely the province of birds. The autumn migration of caribou from arctic Canada south to better feeding grounds is well known as is the movement of salmon up rivers to their spawning grounds. However, there are few examples of animal travel more remarkable than the journeys of the monarch butterfly which take the species from as far north as the Great Lakes south to Mexico for the winter. Unlike bird migration, the whole journey of the monarch butterfly is not performed by the same individual. At the onset of spring, millions of butterflies leave their wintering valley in the Mexican Sierras and fly north, stopping *en route* to mate and lay eggs on milkweed plants. The subsequent generation then continues to journey north and after the process has been repeated several times, monarchs finally reach Toronto. After one brief generation, they embark on the return journey: truly a remarkable feat for an insect.

Maples

As Canada's national emblem, the maple leaf signifies the importance of the tree both to the country's environment and to its economy. Depending upon the species, the wood may be used for timber, the sap can be used to make maple syrup and maple sugar, and the trees themselves are an integral part of Canada's landscape.

In the woods and forest bordering Lake Ontario up to six species of maple may be found growing. By far the most important of these is the sugar maple. As its name implies, it is this species which is most important as a source of sap, the technique for its extraction

The beginning of the fall – the changing colours of maple leaves in early autumn

having first been performed by indigenous Indians. The timber of sugar maple is also important; since it is both hard and strong, it can be used for anything from furniture to veneer.

In the autumn, one of the glories of the deciduous woodlands of southern Canada is the changing colours of the leaves. The colours vary from red to golden yellow depending on the species, and as they cascade on to the woodland floor they create a beautiful mosaic of shape and hue underfoot.

FOOD AND DRINK

Visitors to Toronto will find the same styles in food as they will in any other major city of North America — the basic Anglo-Saxon roast beef, steaks, chops and apple pie, the heritage brought by early settlers overlaid with all the influences of Europe and the rest of the world.

Unfortunately they may never get a taste of cooking which is definitely Canadian because much of it is concentrated in other provinces, and while the pea soup and *tourtière* of Québec found their way west to Ontario long ago, there are dishes such as the Acadian delicacies of New Brunswick which can only be found there. Because Ontario's growing season for fruits and vegetables

Fresh fruit — but mostly imported

is relatively short, it depends upon places such as Mexico, Chile and California for its fresh produce in the winter and there is never a shortage of tomatoes and avocados, passion fruit and cauliflower at any time of the year.

But oh, in summer, the glory of the first sweet and tender corn, the huge vine-ripened tomatoes and the slim asparagus stalks when they finally come out of the fields!

And then comes autumn, the true harvest, time of sweet squash and pumpkin pies, turnips and the sharp crunch of crisp apples. Or those same apples in dumplings of pie dough seeped through with maple syrup and cream. There are overweight Canadians and such dumplings are one reason why, though most feel the game is worth the candle.

One of the oldest and best

FOOD AND DRINK

traditions in Ontario rural communities is the church supper, with ham and scalloped potatoes that are brown and crisp from the oven and platters piled high with corn on the cob, dripping with butter. Apple pie and sharp, well-aged Ontario Cheddar follow . . . and a man could die happy.

But unfortunately, only if you have friends in Toronto or travel extensively through the countryside will you have a reasonable chance of enjoying that meal because it is not something easily found in city restaurants.

Barbecued meals, however, are, and in that respect Toronto restaurants mirror the tastes of the average citizen, for Torontonians spend a lot of time at their backyard barbecues in summer. Having waited so long for warm weather they are determined to squeeze every last drop of enjoyment out of it. And in this — and many other respects — they do not differ significantly from their US neighbours.

To a large degree, the Canadian food experience mirrors that of much of the northern United States, although you will be assured of getting a decent cup of tea (poured from a teapot) instead of a cup of lukewarm water and a tea bag on the side. But even there, it must be admitted that with the exception of a few of the city's elegant hotels there is no such thing as afternoon tea, unless you drive into the surrounding countryside and hunt down a tearoom.

While most Torontonians would agree that food is expensive, the city is in the midst of a love affair with convenience foods — not simply fast foods (although there are all the usual chain operations) but fantastic gourmet ready-to-heat foods sold for equally fantastic prices. Toronto's restaurant menus cover the world, with the cuisine of France and Italy being by far the strongest and the most recent trend coming from California. There is no shortage of domestic beer (which is like German and Dutch beer in strength and taste) nor of imported beer, and there is never a problem in choosing a good bottle of wine to accompany your meal. The problem may arise when you go to pay the bill, for mark-ups on wine, first by the government, then by the restaurants, can be horrendous.

Unfortunately, you cannot beat the system, for it is illegal to 'brown-bag' it (arrive with your favourite bottle of plonk under your arm) as you can in, say, Sydney or sections of New York city, and, given Ontario's greed for sin taxes, the practice will never be condoned. Happily, an increasing number of places will now let you order by the glass and you can always fall back on a carafe of the house wine.

Eating Out

Interest in food seems to be at an all-time high in Toronto with trendy new restaurants opening every few weeks. That is partly due to the fact that it is a big, still growing city, with tastes influenced by immigrants, and partly to the fact that like many North American cities it has a populace that is growing more adventurous in its eating habits. It is no problem to find a restaurant in Toronto. After all, there are more than 5,000 of them. But making recommendations can be a problem. New stars can rise quickly, find favour for a little while and wane just as quickly. And in the case of many of the city's new breed of young chefs, by the time you arrive to check out the rave reviews, he or she has decamped to follow a new path. For that reason some new spots have been omitted from the

Every opportunity is taken to enjoy refreshment al fresco

following listings, which concentrate on places that are not only superb in themselves but stand an excellent chance of being still in business when a reader wants a dinner. (Ideally, one should complement this list with the latest reviews in *Toronto Life* magazine and in two of the major newspapers, *The Toronto Star* and the *Globe & Mail*, whose listings can change by the week as the chefs wax and wane.)

Most Toronto restaurants are open for lunch but some are not, so it is always wise to check. The usual dinner hours run roughly from 19.00 to 22.00 although many restaurants stay open later at weekends. Many

FOOD AND DRINK

close on Sundays so again, phone ahead. And, as always, reservations are needed at just about all the better places. Again, while most restaurants accept a variety of credit cards, it is wise to make sure they will honour your particular brand (especially in some of the smaller eateries).

The service charge is not included in Toronto and tipping in the region of 10 to 15 per cent (before the 8 per cent Ontario sales tax) is appropriate.

NORTH AMERICAN

Beaujolais, 165 John Street (tel: 598-4656). Probably at the height of its well-deserved popularity and with a menu that owes much to California. There is a wealth of avocado, pesto, roasted red and yellow peppers and superbly prepared entrées. Worth a visit for the sheer delight of a sampler plate of starters called Great Beginnings. And since they also offer a plate containing no less than six luscious desserts it is wise to take a friend along. Closed on Sundays. Moderate prices.

Bloor Street Diner, 50 Bloor Street West (tel: 928-3105). Well situated for uptown shopping binges, this is high-tech dining with a vengeance. Choice recorded jazz in the background and burgers to match, along with speedy service. Open all week, 11.00 to 03.00. Moderate prices.

Fred's Not Here, 321 King Street West (tel: 971-9155). Popular with theatre-goers, puts an emphasis on smoked or grilled entrées − game, Brome Lake

duck and swordfish are a few − prepared and served with aplomb. Imaginative décor and pleasant service but, since it is one of the city's new and popular eateries, be sure to leave enough time if you are intent on making the opening curtain. Moderate prices.

Hart's, 225 Church Street (tel: 368-5350). Relaxed and casual with good daily specials chalked around the walls at handy intervals. A no-nonsense menu includes pastas, hearty soups, burgers and a first-rate Caesar salad. Friendly staff and always a clutch of regulars at the bar. Closed on Sundays. Inexpensive.

Metropolis, 838 Yonge Street (tel: 924-4100). One of the few places for the Canadian touch, they're doing inventive things with Oka and St Benoit cheese atop onion and cider soup, wild rice puddings and Huron

*An Atlantic Canadian dish,
breaded rabbit with rice*

Country rabbit. And for a taste of Canada, Ontario-style, try the Upper Canada Ale and Creemore Springs Lager. Highly recommended. Closed on Sundays. Inexpensive.

CONTINENTAL/ INTERNATIONAL

Bemelmans, 83 Bloor Street West (tel: 960-0306). With its polished wood, brass, marble and glass it is somewhere between a chophouse and a private club and although there is a large and varied menu, it is the bar scene that is the big draw. An outdoor patio for the summer months and civilised hours for nighthawks. Mon-Fri: 11.30 to 03.00. Sat: 11.00 to 03.00. Sun: 11.00 to midnight. Inexpensive.

Bistro 990, 990 Bay Street (tel: 921-9990). Across from the Sutton Place Hotel and close to the movers and shakers of Queen's Park, it is basically a sophisticated bistro, all arches and terracotta and cathedral ceiling. Appealing *à la carte*, with an emphasis on fresh, simply prepared dishes, delicate iced soups in summer and a wealth of good desserts. There is also a *prix fixe* menu which will keep you happy through four courses. Expensive.

Café Victoria (King Edward Hotel) 37 King Street East (tel: 863-9700). Sunday brunch may never taste this good again. The board groans with beef Wellington, lamb, roast pork and cold turkey. Pâtés and egg dishes and a profusion of breads and rolls almost complete the picture. (Leave room for fresh fruits and cheesecake.) The stylish elegance of this grand hotel adds to the enjoyment. Inexpensive.

Courtyard Café, 22 St Thomas Street (tel: 979-2212). Still one of the places to see and be seen and if there are movie stars in town you can bet on it they will end up here at least once. A big sky-lit room with food which, although it can be uneven, is always beautifully prepared. *Cuisine naturelle* as well as heavier fare, justly famed ices and fresh fruit sorbets and a series of late-night snacks to keep the table-hoppers going. Sunday brunch, too. Expensive.

The Daily Planet, 40 Eglinton Avenue East (tel: 440-0030). Big and casual with a menu to match, it is handily placed for shopping on north Yonge St and

FOOD AND DRINK

popular for late night snacks after the movies. The Sunday brunch crowd staked it out as a bargain long ago, so get there early to avoid queues. Open until 01.00 Mon-Sat and from 11.30 to 23.00 on Sundays. Inexpensive.

Ed's Warehouse Restaurant, 270 King Street West adjacent to the Royal Alexandra Theatre (tel: 593-6676). When Ed Mirvish does anything he does it with style and verve. Thanks to him the Royal Alex was saved some years ago and, more recently, he has given new life to London's Old Vic. The Warehouse is pure show biz with 400 Tiffany lamps, 1,300 seats and signed photos of all the greats who have appeared at the Royal Alex over the years and it is chock-a-block with antiques. Prime roast beef and steaks are served and the enjoyment and value cannot be topped. Inexpensive.

Right next door are **Ed's Chinese, Ed's Italian, Ed's Seafood** and **Old Ed's** — again, excellent value and good fun. Dress codes have been abandoned (there was a time when no tie meant positively no admittance). No reservations taken unless you happen to be a party of 20 or more. Mon-Sat: noon to 14.00, 17.00 to 22.00; Sun: 17.00 to 21.00. Inexpensive.

Fenton's, 2 Gloucester Street (tel: 961-8485). Three rooms make up one of the city's most distinguished restaurants. The Front Room with its parlour-type loveseats, glowing fire in winter and masses of fresh flowers is a sophisticated café at its very best. It shares its menu with the Garden Room, a wonder of

Ed's Warehouse — or maybe Ed's Chinese, Ed's Italian, Ed's Seafood or Old Ed's?

glass and foliage with more armfuls of unstudied flowers and twinkling lights in the trees as dusk falls. The Cream of Leek soup with Stilton has been on the menu since it first opened — don't miss it. The Downstairs Room is more casual and easier on the wallet but still done with style. Expensive.

Glossops, 39 Prince Arthur Avenue (tel: 964-2440). Well situated for Yorkville's galleries and boutiques, it is a nicely converted house with a chef who likes to surprise the palate. Perhaps a soy and rice vinegar accompaniment to grilled salmon, or a mix of sage and walnuts. Closed on Sundays. Expensive.

Jennie's, 360 Queen Street East (tel: 861-1461). Art Deco prints, a cosy atmosphere and a young chef with an inventive mind which dwells sometimes on the Orient. Curried Bombay shrimp

and beef teriaki can share the table with delicious garlic cheese bread. Sunday brunch and patio dining in the summer. Moderate prices.

Panama Joe's, 124 Danforth Avenue (tel: 463-0085). Go for lunch if you are in a tropical mood. A live palm, lots of bamboo and Mexican artwork along with some of the best corned beef sandwiches in town, as well as up-market pastas and calamari. At night the dance crowd hits the scene. Open until 01.00 Monday to Saturday. Moderate prices.

Rotterdam, 600 King Street West (tel: 868-6882). Crowded watering hole, noisy, but alive, with a menu featuring beef and chicken along with seafoods and salads. Pick your way through a huge list of beers and consult with friendly servers. Moderate prices.

Scaramouche, 1 Benvenuto Place (tel: 961-8011). It has been the stamping ground for many of Toronto's new breed of young, innovative chefs and its lustre is undimmed. Creative cooking with a French slant and superb desserts, all enjoyed over a spectacular view of the city. Good pasta bar (less expensive) in the adjacent lounge. Closed on Sundays. Very expensive.

CHINESE

Champion House, 478 Dundas Street West (tel: 977-8282). For lovers of the fiery Szechuan style, plus spectacular Peking duck. Large menu and the waiters really hustle. Closed on Tuesdays. Moderate prices.

Great Wall, 442-444 Spadina

Avenue (tel: 961-5554). Big and crowded but a goodly selection of three types of Chinese cooking. A good spot for enjoyment if you are with a large party — alone you may never be heard over the din. Very inexpensive.

Pink Pearl, 120 Avenue Road (tel: 966-3631). Uptown chic in the Cantonese manner. Nicely served as befits the surroundings. Pick your way through the many *dim sum* offerings after you have broken your bank at the Hazelton Lanes boutiques. Moderate prices.

Sai Woo, 130 Dundas Street West (tel: 977-4988). An institution of Chinatown with a menu that never ends.

Traditional Cantonese style cooking. Excellent pickerel. Inexpensive.

DANISH

Copenhagen Room, 101 Bloor Street West (tel: 920-3287). Walk into this comfortable restaurant and the murals of Copenhagen envelop you. Sixty types of open-faced sandwiches, hearty entrées and authentic Danish pastry. Sip an ice cold aquavit or a Tuborg and make a firm date for the regular Tuesday night traditional Danish buffet. Consistently good. Closed on

Toronto's Chinatown, the third largest in North America, has more than 100 Chinese restaurants

Sundays. Moderate prices.
At street level there's the **Danish Food Centre** (tel: 920-5505). Small, cafeteria-style and with the same wonderful sandwiches, salads and pastries. They also do a brisk take-away trade. Inexpensive.

FRENCH

Arlequin, 134 Avenue Road (tel: 928-9521). Elegant but relaxed restaurant in which to enjoy food with an accent on the south of France. Also a first-rate stop if you're buying food for a picnic; its succulent pâtés, quiches and unusual salads are available to take away. Attentive service. Closed on Mondays. Moderate prices.

Auberge Gavroche, 90 Avenue Road (tel: 920-0956). In one of the few remaining lovely old houses on this part of the street, the setting is serene and the classic food rarely disappoints. Its menu and that of **l'Entrecôte,** the less expensive upstairs bistro, can be sampled on the front patio during the summer. Closed on Sundays. Moderate prices.

Le Bistingo, 349 Queen Street West (tel: 598-3490). Exquisite food prepared with a minimum of fuss and accompanied by sauces that show a masterly hand in the kitchen. Top marks for service and a well-deserved reputation. Closed on Sundays. Expensive.

Bofinger Brasserie, 1507 Yonge Street (tel: 923-2300). An uptown Parisienne brasserie with the prerequisite Impressionist prints and fresh flowers. Good fish dishes and excellent steak and *pommes frites.* Get there early

for lunch as it is a popular spot for nearby office workers. Moderate prices.

La Bodega, 30 Baldwin Street (tel: 977-1287). The atmosphere is comfortable with lace curtains adding a homey touch and a regular clientele which has been coming back for years. Splendid entrecôtes, tender lamb and fresh fish as well as a dessert menu with some of the best profiteroles outside France. A short walk from the Art Gallery of Ontario. Closed on Sundays. Moderate prices.

Les Copains, 48 Wellington Street East (tel: 869-0898). Upstairs. Handy for the O'Keefe Centre and the St Lawrence Centre for the Performing Arts. Comfortably stylish with dishes like sautéed loin of lamb with smooth madeira sauce and interesting vegetables. Take advantage of its pre-theatre menu. Closed on Sundays. Moderate prices.

Corner House, 501 Davenport Road (tel: 923-2604). With Casa Loma towering on the rise above, you can set your own scene for a romantic evening. The Victorian house offers five intimate little rooms where the chef serves up food in the classic manner. Knowledgeable and very personal service. Closed on Sundays. Expensive.

La Grenouille, 2837 Yonge Street (tel: 481-3093). A wide selection of regional bistro dishes and helpful waiters who do not sneer at a less than masterful touch with the French. Duck and veal and garlicked frogs' legs as well as flavourful tarts and parfaits. Closed on Sundays. Inexpensive.

FOOD AND DRINK

Le Select Bistro, 328 Queen Street West (tel: 596-6405). It is so tiny they suspend the bread baskets over the tables. Always crowded and jolly with folk tucking into *moules marinière* or steak and frites. Good bistro food and an extensive wine list. Moderate price.

Winston's, 104 Adelaide Street West (tel: 363-1627). Sometimes likened to Maxim's, this shrine to the Establishment is home to politicians and top businessmen who hold court at lunch. As you would expect, outstandingly good food and service to match an awe-inspiring wine list. Closed on Sundays. Very expensive.

Top people eat at Winston's

GREEK

Anesty's, 16 Church Street (tel: 368-1881). A lot bigger than the average Greek taverna but the whitewashed walls, trees and hanging brass lamps aid the illusion. Excellent starters, sometimes uneven entrées. Closed on Sundays. Inexpensive.

Pappas Grill, 440 Danforth Avenue (tel: 469-9595). Unlike the majority of the many small Greek restaurants in the area Pappas adds pastas, pizzas and burgers to its menu and while they are good, it is probably the lamb and the *dolmades* which draw the crowds. Moderate prices.

The Palace, 722 Pape Avenue (tel: 463-3393). Always popular, with its seafood often singled out for special praise, it somehow manages to leave you feeling relaxed despite its rush of people. Moderate prices.

Penelope, 33 Yonge Street (tel: 947-1159). Handy for the O'Keefe Centre and with all the appropriate mainstays of a Greek menu. Perhaps a little less relaxed than its Danforth Avenue cousins but friendly and consistent. Closed on Sundays. Moderate prices.

ITALIAN

Barolo, 193 Carlton Street (tel: 961-4747). Northern Italian cuisine concentrating on simple, well-prepared food. Superbly grilled meats and unexpected additions to the gnocchi make for a pleasant meal in lively surroundings. Closed on Sundays. Moderate prices.

La Bruschetta, 1325 St Clair Avenue West (tel: 656-8622). Typical of the many small restaurants in the part of the city known as Little Italy. Spaghetti, minestrone, veal and salad, plus some unusual dishes you may never have tried before. The staff are eager to explain and recommend. Closed Sundays. Moderate prices.

Centro, 2472 Yonge Street (tel: 483-2211). A combination of Northern Italy and California in

A classic Italian meal —
pasta, red wine and salad

the food and maybe in the décor, too. Once you get your mind on the menu you will find excellent pastas, shellfish and a wonderful fresh sorbet and fruit platter. A spectacular wine list and one that is priced for good value. Phone ahead because the place draws big crowds. Very expensive.

Cibo, 1055 Yonge Street (tel: 921-2166). Neighbourhood restaurant for the high society Rosedale crowd. Great people-watching but with long queues as the price of success. A menu that could be called new-wave Italian — sliced cold veal and tuna dressed with a brandy mayonnaise, fresh lobster with passion fruit, etc. Daily blackboard specials of fish and pasta dishes. Reservations a must. Fast service — don't expect to linger. Moderate prices.

Il Monello, 1392 Yonge Street (tel: 968-0030). Elegant Italian with a decidedly French accent. Perhaps Boston bluefish or red snapper grilled with a herbed butter, good *bruschetta* for starters and smoothly sauced fresh pastas. Highly praised desserts. Moderate prices.

Oggi Bistro, 254 Eglinton Avenue East (tel: 489-3777). Spend a morning in the antique shops of Mount Pleasant and you can lunch in this gracious family-owned-and-run restaurant. Pastas, chicken and seafood in a relaxed atmosphere. Closed Sundays. Moderate prices.

Orso, 106 St John Street (tel: 596-1989). What was once a blacksmith's premises now houses what many reckon to be one of the city's best eateries. Slightly austere décor but the hand-painted service plates and innovative food bring it all to life. Chic pizzas on the lunch menu and quietly efficient service. Closed on Sundays. Expensive.

La Scala restaurant: fine house, fine food − and prices to match

La Scala, 1121 Bay Street (tel: 964-7100). In an elegant old house, a stone's throw from the shops of the ManuLife Centre and Bloor Street. Long established. Always formal but never flashy and with food to match. Excellent service and a fairly wide-ranging wine list. Closed on Sundays. Very expensive.

Trattoria Giancarlo, 41 Clinton Street (tel: 533-9619). Casual and comfortable with fresh pastas, sauces and well-grilled seafood. And what every self-respecting neighbourhood trattoria should have, a small front patio for summertime dining. Closed Sundays and Mondays. Moderate prices.

JAPANESE

Furusato, 401 Bloor Street East (tel: 967-0180). A happy blend of Japanese and French cuisine known as (what else?) Frapanese, which combines the best of both. Much to choose from a first-class menu in tastefully decorated surroundings. Closed on Sundays.
Moderate prices.

Katsura, 900 York Mills Road in the Prince Hotel (tel: 444-2511). This is a showplace for all that is exquisite in Japanese culture and food. *Teppanyaki* chefs do their stuff and the *sushi* and *tempura* counters do brisk trade. Expensive.

Sasaya, 257 Eglinton Avenue West (tel: 487-3508). Good *sushi* and *tempura* bars and a large menu which often needs explanation unless you are an expert. Fortunately you will have help from an efficient and friendly staff.
Inexpensive.

SEAFOOD

Filet of Sole, 11 Duncan Street (tel: 598-3256). Near the Metro Toronto Convention Centre and the theatre district. Fresh fish and lobster daily along with oysters shucked at Henry's Oyster Bar. Very extensive menu which includes steak and

chicken. Lots of fun and casual, but not so much so that you don't need reservations.
Moderate prices.

Josos, 202 Davenport Road (tel: 925-1903). Exotic nudes adorn the walls of this intimate Mediterranean-style restaurant and between the food and the atmosphere it is hard not to have a good time. Pricey, but with large portions of fresh, grilled fish, deep fried calamari and pastas. Closed on Sundays. Expensive.

The Old Fish Market, 12 Market Street (tel: 363-0334). Popular with St Lawrence Market shoppers and any number of nearby business people, this bustling place is best approached on foot or by taxi. Satisfying, with fresh catches of the day (menus are printed twice daily), an oyster bar and good seafood. Vegetables are sometimes not all they might be. Inexpensive.

Phebe's, 641 Mount Pleasant Road (tel: 484-6428). An oyster bar and friendly neighbourhood restaurant. Service can be a bit hit-or-miss but even JR Ewing would approve mightily of the Texas barbecued shrimp and luscious pies. Closed on Sundays. Inexpensive.

Trata, 1055 Yonge Street (tel: 924-1257). Choose a fish and pay by weight or order from the menu, either way you will get a well prepared meal. Cheerful checkered tablecloths and wood floors give a tavern-like feeling. Share some of the oozing baklava for dessert. Closed on Sundays. Inexpensive.

FOOD AND DRINK

The Whistling Oyster, 11 Duncan Street (tel: 598-7707). In the basement of Filet of Sole. An informal place with a popular bar thronged with singles. Seafood and lots of pastas. Inexpensive.

STEAKHOUSE

Barberian's, 7 Elm Street (tel: 597-0335). Arguably the best place for the noble sirloin, T-bones and Barberian's own Delmonico cut, perfectly served by knowing waiters. No-fuss dressing on the Caesar salad and the apple beignets with ice cream are mouthwatering. Open until 01.00 Monday–Saturday. Sundays until midnight.
Expensive.

Carman's Dining Club, 26 Alexander Street (tel: 924-8697). Excellent steaks but you have to be a lover of garlic because it is laid on with a heavy hand. Within walking distance of Maple Leaf Gardens where National Hockey League games, rock concerts and recitals are held.
Expensive.

El Toro, 39 Colborne Street behind the King Edward Hotel (tel: 368-2418). All the mandatory steakhouse fare at fairly reasonable prices but it is included here mainly for **Nicky's,** its upstairs pub-like lounge where you can find great steak pies and what some believe to be the best steak sandwiches in the city. Closed on Sundays. Very inexpensive.

Gatsby's, 504 Church Street (tel: 925-4545). An elegant Victorian era dining room, all glittering gilt and chandeliers. Steaks are what they do best but there is a whole range of other Continental dishes, too. Near Maple Leaf Gardens. Closed on Sundays. Expensive.

George Bigliardi's, 463 Church Street (tel: 922-9594). In the Italian manner. Attractive atmosphere with a variety of veal and seafood, too. Dependable steaks and excellent Caesar salads. Open for dinner only. Closed Sundays. Mon-Sat. 17.00 to 00.30. Expensive.

SWISS

Bistro Bernard, 6 St Joseph Street (tel: 926-1900). A quiet place to escape the rigours of Yonge Street. Rich soups made richer with the addition of mounded cream, delicious rossti potatoes, roast lamb and the like. Closed on Sundays. Inexpensive.

Mövenpick, 165 York Street (tel: 366-5234). Only the Swiss could run a chain this well. The place is large — actually three distinct areas in one — with the formal Rossli being the most expensive. Sit up at the wine bar (offering rare wines by the glass) or in the surrounding Belle Terrasse to enjoy authentic Swiss food. The bread is baked daily and special menus are themed to seasonal produce. The Sunday brunch buffet is always packed. Mon-Sat: 07.30 to 01.00; Sun: 07.30 to midnight. Inexpensive. There is also a Mövenpick at 129 Yorkville Ave. No Sunday brunch but they cater to uptown nighthawks Mon-Fri: 07.30 to 02.00 and Sat-Sun: 07.30 to 01.00.

SHOPPING

Any visitor in the grip of the
'shop till you drop' syndrome
will feel at home in Toronto
where every opportunity is
afforded to spend, spend.
Whatever you are after, it is
here somewhere in the city's
shopping centres, boutiques
and markets, the ubiquitous
suburban malls, or the
individual shops of its
neighbourhoods. However, it is
no duty-free paradise. You pay
the going rate and you get
quality. There are department
stores such as Eaton's, Simpsons
and The Bay for middle-of-the-
roaders. Holt Renfrew and
Creeds cater to the carriage
trade and for big spenders
there is a wealth of branches of

internationally renowned
companies and imports from all
over the world.
There are lots of items made in
Canada but Eskimo soapstone
carving makes the most
uniquely Canadian memento or
gift. But be alert. There are
many imitations and inferior
works around so look carefully
before you buy.
High on anyone's list of places to
shop are the more than 300
shops and services of **The Eaton
Centre,** designed along the
lines of Milan's Galleria, all
soaring glass and light, and one
of Toronto's top tourist
attractions.
It is anchored north and south
by Eaton's and Simpsons, and
Michael Snow's sculpted flock of
Canada geese hovers high
under the arched glass of the
roof.
(Beautiful as they are,

Eaton's store in the Eaton Centre,
a must for all shoppers

Sculpted Canada geese hover over shoppers beneath the arched glass roof of the Eaton Centre

Torontonians seemed to be taking them for granted until a few years ago when the Centre's publicists decided to festoon them with red ribbons at Christmas. Such a howl arose from the artist and public that the geese were returned to their unadorned splendour in short order.)

The Centre is easily reached by subway, bus or streetcar and there is a mind-boggling variety of things to buy and do, as well as some of the best fast food and speciality snacking in the city.

The Eaton Centre is, of course,

just one of many ways to dive into Toronto's **underground city** with its more than 1,000 shops, restaurants, nightclubs, movie theatres and other facilities. At its north end the underground begins at The Atrium on Bay, from which it runs south beneath the Eaton Centre, Simpsons, the Sheraton Centre, First Canadian Place, the Toronto Dominion Centre and the Royal York Hotel, ending, or beginning, as the case may be, at Union Station.

On any given day there are masses of people eating, banking, buying clothes or shoes or television sets, seeing their doctors or dentists, stocking up on groceries or just indulging in dinner and a movie.

Apart from all of that, the underground is a marvellous way to escape the snows and winds of winter and the moist heat of midsummer.

(In winter people have been known to drive their heated cars out of their heated garages in the morning, arrive downtown and park in underground garages, take elevators to their offices, dive underground for lunch, then reverse their trips at day's end, never having felt the nip of frost. Or, in summer, the enervating heat of a humid day.)

Queen's Quay Terminal on the water's edge at Harbourfront contains many small boutiques and speciality shops, some of the best novelty items in the city and excellent food. If you want to take a gourmet picnic over to the Toronto Islands (and you should), stock up here.

There is a large number of imports in the shops, together with much that is Canadian. Do not miss the **Tilley Endurables** shop for safari-style clothing for men and women. It is nicely designed and exceptionally well made. So well made, in fact, that the labels on many items carry the succinct washing instructions: 'Give 'em hell'.

This may just be the most glamorous building in Toronto. For years it was known as the terminal warehouse, built, in 1926, like a fortress.

So much like a fortress that when the developers came along, a few years back, they decided it was easier to convert it and stack high-priced luxury condominiums on its roof than demolish it.

A short walk from there and you're at the **Harbourfront Antique Market,** Canada's largest and not to be missed. It is so big that you can spend the better part of a day there if you are really an antique hound.

Bloor-Yorkville
Bloor Street West, from Yonge Street to Avenue Road, offers a run of shops that carry all the good things in life, so much so that one would need a whole book just to list them. But here are a few, to set the tone:
The ManuLife Centre, 55 Bloor Street West. Home to **Creeds** (where the assistants are so well dressed it is hard to tell them from their customers), plus two levels of shops which include **Marks and Spencer** and **Birks,** a major Canadian jewellery firm. **William Ashley,** 50 Bloor Street

West, sells premium china, silver and crystal at sharply discounted prices and the selection is incredible. If Ashley's does not carry it, it probably has not been made.
Clothesline, 50 Bloor Street West, second level. Take a breather from European designer labels and look at these well-tailored Canadian examples. Vibrant clothes and accessories from Canadian designer **Marilyn Brooks** are also on this level. Do not miss them if you want something that is up to or way ahead of the times.
Davids, 66 Bloor Street West, Shoes and boots from Jourdan and Maud Frizon, among others. Top prices but watch for frequent sales.
Georg Jensen, 95A Bloor Street West. Across from the Danish Food Centre. Furniture upstairs and Royal Copenhagen china everywhere, but it is the classic silver jewellery which is always the real Jensen showstopper.
Harry Rosen, 80 Bloor Street West. Huge selections of elegant men's wear at this stylish outfitters (also caters for women).
Holt Renfrew, 50 Bloor Street West. High fashion for women with Canadian exclusives on many of Europe's best designers (for which you will need a 'price is no object' attitude) plus men's and children's wear. The café on the top floor is a prime spot for tired shoppers.
The Irish Shop, 110 Bloor Street West. Some of the best and brightest in Irish design here, along with tableware and books.

Separate entrance to the men's store.
A short walk north on Avenue Road and you are in the midst of Yorkville, an enclave of exclusivity which embraces Yorkville and Hazleton Avenues, Cumberland and Scollard Streets and part of Avenue Road.
Back in the days when the flower children held their brief reign this area was full of hippies, folk artists, coffee houses and more than a few illegal substances. It was beguiling, of a summer's evening, to wander around, stop for coffee, and wonder at the kids.
Now the place holds the heartbeat of café society — and is still the best place in town for people-watching, although now the streets are lined with

Examples of Eskimo painting and sculpture on display at the Innuit Gallery of Eskimo Art

expensive cars and the jeans have designer labels.

The old townhouses of Yorkville Avenue have been renovated to house chic boutiques and galleries, the restaurants are legion and in the summer months the sidewalk cafés sprout bright umbrellas.

Hazelton Lanes, 55 Avenue Road. An elegant complex full of boutiques around a posh outdoor restaurant (dismantled in winter to make way for a skating rink).

The Compleat Kitchen, 87 Yorkville Avenue. Utensils, gadgets, cookbooks — just about anything that can (or should) be used in a well set-up kitchen can be found here.

Fetoun, 97 Scollard Street, Antique lace, Persian rugs, a chandelier and a statue of Anna Pavlova adorn this opulent four-storey monument to *haute couture.* Fabulous ball gowns and classic suits emanate from the workroom and even most of the off-the-peg is one of a kind.

The General Store, Hazelton Lanes, lower level. Great place for gift-shopping with everything from kitchenware to bathrobes, books and glassware to . . . well, just about anything you can think of.

Innuit Gallery of Eskimo Art, 9 Prince Arthur Avenue. Perhaps the best place in the city to see beautiful examples and get some idea of what to look for when you are ready to buy.

Irene Dale, 9 Yorkville Avenue. Canadian-designed children's clothing with a beautiful attention to detail, colour and an awareness of a child's activities.

Mirvish Village, Markham Street south of Bloor, a block west of Bathurst Street. The same Mirvish of theatrical and restaurant fame (see **Eating Out**) has made this little block of Victoriana a pleasant place to stroll, shop for antiques, collectables, art and books, or enjoy a meal. At the north end, where the streets intersect, stands the cornerstone of his empire, **Honest Ed's,** the blockbuster of all bargain stores. It's big, it's tacky, it's got the world's largest electric sign on its roof and just getting around in it can be like going the wrong way on an escalator, but if you are feeling really strong, there are definite bargains to be had.

Going West

Queen Street West, west from McCaul Street over to Bathurst Street. This area has the city's most avant-garde flavour and it is where the artists and musicians hang out. The fashions (in the shops and on the street) are outrageous and there is a lot of pink hair, black leather and new wave. But there are bookstores, record stores, vintage clothing shops and many exceedingly good cafés and restaurants, too. Don't miss it.

Village by the Grange, 49 McCaul Street. Hard by the Art Gallery of Ontario, this complex contains over 60 shops and boutiques and five restaurants. You can buy everything from personalised stationery to exotic birds and it is a good place for unusual gift shops. There is also an international food market with 25 kiosks selling tastes from all over the world. Free parking underground, evenings and weekends.

Markets

Kensington Market. This is a delight which was born in the early part of the century and survives to this day, despite the occasional short-lived plan to knock it down and build something tidier and antiseptic. Bounded by Bathurst Street and Spadina Avenue and Dundas and College Streets, it sprawls over a residential area which in 1815 was a place of wide sweeping lawns. Fifty years later the land had been split up and British immigrants arrived to take up residence. There was no market in their time but after them came Jews from Europe, for whom markets were essential, and by the 1930s the Kensington was flourishing. Hungarian and Italian immigrants had their innings but by far the biggest influence since the original Jewish impetus was that of the Portuguese, who arrived from the Azores in the 1950s and who now account for at least half the area's population.

Today, with their blessing, Augusta Street throbs with soulful *fado* music, the wares from the tiny shops and stalls spill over what passes for pavements and everywhere there is life and vitality.

The market also attracts the West Indian community, just to the south and recently the Koreans and Vietnamese have joined the fray.

(It is hard to understand the reasoning but some people are intrepid enough to actually drive through Kensington's cramped and crowded streets. As the no parking signs in New York city say: 'Don't even think about it'. Much better to be an innocent observer as the horns start hooting and the jostling for every inch of every illegal parking space begins.)

St Lawrence Market, 92 Front Street East (corner of Front and Jarvis Streets). The best in produce, fish, poultry and meat is available here, as well as cheese, breads and other foodstuffs. But even if you do not want to shop for groceries, it is well worthwhile wandering around while you enjoy a cup of coffee and one of the hot Canadian-bacon-on-a-bun sandwiches sold by several food stalls. On Saturdays the market across the street adds another 60 stalls to the mix.

The Neighbourhoods

And then there are Toronto's many neighbourhoods, each as different as the citizens' ethnic backgrounds, but all with one thing in common — interesting shopping and walking areas. It would take up far too much space in this book (and be needlessly repetitive) to list shops within each area. Suffice

Shop window in the Beaches, a good area for original shops

it to say all the neighbourhoods contain them along with restaurants and cafés and each is well worth a visitor's time, not only for the shops themselves, but to gain some knowledge of what holds the city together.

The Beaches. One of the most relaxed areas of the city, with access to the waterfront, its parks, boardwalk and lovely houses are reminders of the past. It retains the allure it once had as Toronto's long-ago summer retreat, despite booming property values. Shopping is eclectic and original.

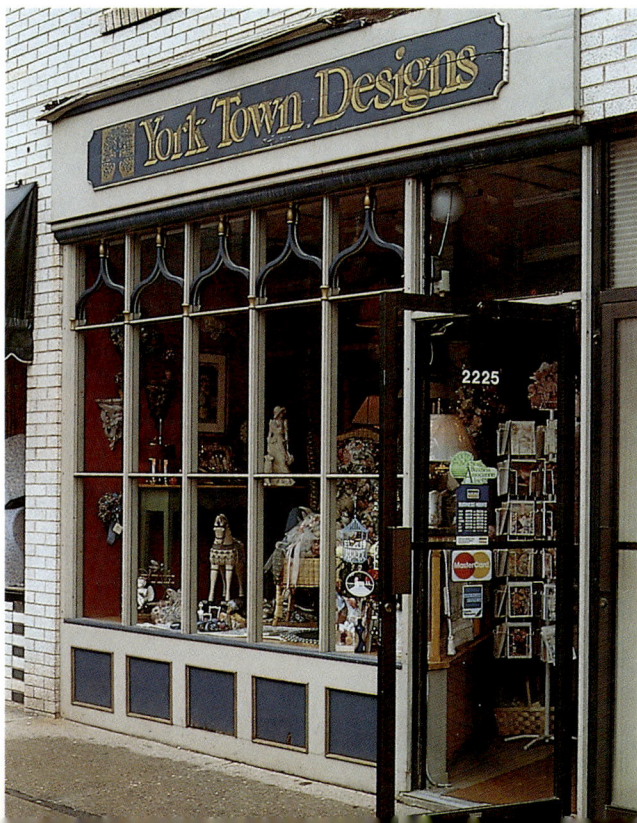

SHOPPING

Make for Queen Street East, between just east of Woodbine Avenue and along to Victoria Park Avenue and you will find folk art, Oriental rugs, junk stores, bookshops, cafés and some good British-type pubs. Wander through some of the residential streets if you have time and you will see everything from mock-Tudor on tiny cottages to imposing Victorian beauties.

Bloor West Village at Jane and Bloor Streets. A real riches-to-rags-to-riches story happened here when the east-west subway line made downtown shopping easily accessible in 1966. What had been a vital part of the community quickly went into decline as people deserted the neighbourhood for the bigger city stores.

Businesses closed down and the street was rapidly sliding into a slum when a few owners decided to fight back by funding a revitalisation scheme with higher business taxes. Today the markets, delicatessens, pastry shops, high fashion and antique stores are not only filled with residents, but they are a magnet for shoppers from all over Toronto. More European than North American with influences from all over that continent, the wide tree-lined street is once again bustling, the cafés and gift shops filled with people. (Easily reached by subway and a stone's throw from High Park.)

Chinatown, west of Spadina Avenue to Bay Street, College Street to south of Dundas Street.

The third largest Chinatown in North America (San Francisco and New York are the leaders), this one had its origins in 1878. The shops, stalls and restaurants are always bustling but on Saturdays and Sundays things go into top gear — it seems that every member of this large community is out shopping, eating or just gossiping over a counter.

It is a place of bakeries and herbalists, fish and meat markets, craft stores and clothing and, of course, many restaurants. There was a time when Chinese food in Toronto meant Cantonese food but these days a Chinese meal is just as likely to be Hunan or Szechuan and there are more than a hundred restaurants from which to choose.

The Danforth, between the Don Valley and Woodbine Avenue. If you cannot find a first-class Greek meal on the stretch near Pape Avenue you may have no taste buds. There are fish markets and fruit markets and the bouzouki music pours out on to the street. The only thing that is not completely reminiscent of Athens is the traffic.

Little Italy or Westclair, St Clair Avenue West and Dufferin Street area. When Italy took home the World Cup in 1982 there were reckoned to be half a million Italians out celebrating in this area. Go there for the pastas in the little family-owned restaurants or the hot sausage sandwiches or settle into one of the many sidewalk cafés on a balmy summer evening and enjoy what may be the world's best ice cream.

ACCOMMODATION

Toronto has well over 24,000 hotel rooms but there are times when it is hard to find one, especially in the summer months when the ranks of vacationers and businessmen are swelled by thousands of conventioneers.

The range of hotels runs from luxury in the grand manner to smaller establishments with efficiency (kitchenette) units. It is also possible to find B&B accommodation (see Tight Budget section page 105). Toronto's hotels are scattered across the city, from downtown to the suburbs, and to help

Choose a downtown hotel to be at the heart of the city

make some sense out of it all, the following selective listings are broken into general areas. For a complete listing of all Toronto hotels call Accommodation Toronto on 596-7117. Hours of operation: 15 May to 1 September: 09.00 to 21.00, seven days a week. 2 September to 14 May: Mon-Fri: 09.00 to 21.00. Weekends until 18.00.

The average cost of a double room in Metro Toronto's hotels runs between $75 and $125 for, say, Holiday Inn-style accommodation and from $160 and up for luxury hotels such as the Harbour Castle Westin. Because prices change constantly the following listings indicate only the general range into which each hotel's room rates fall:

ACCOMMODATION

Downtown

Chestnut Park Hotel, 108 Chestnut Street West (tel: 977-5000). Brand new (February 1989) 522-room hotel by City Hall's Nathan Phillips Square. Complete recreation facilities include indoor pool, health club and gymnasium. One of the world's few hotels to be connected to a museum – the Canadian Museum for Textiles, with ceremonial cloths, carpets, etc from around the world, with emphasis on China. Moderately priced.

Delta Chelsea Inn, 33 Gerrard Street West (tel: 595-1975). Some kitchenettes in this 997-room hostelry. Special attention to children with a Creative Centre for those aged three to eight and a kids-style menu in the dining room where those under six eat free. The Chelsea Bun lounge is noted for excellent jazz. Good value. Moderately priced.

Hampton Court Hotel, 415 Jarvis Street (tel: 924-6631). Unusual for downtown Toronto, it is a low-rise 163-room complex built around a central courtyard and swimming pool. Free guest parking. Moderately priced.

Harbour Castle Westin, 1 Harbour Square (tel: 869-1600). A luxurious hotel with 967 rooms, a terraced swimming pool, patio and jogging track and a revolving restaurant, the Lighthouse, perched on its roof offering spectacular views. Very popular hotel and comfortable, despite the fact that it has an entrance that is almost hidden from pedestrians. Expensive.

Hilton International Toronto, 145 Richmond Street West (tel: 869-3456). This 601-room hotel is the home of Trader Vic's (well worth a visit if you feel like exotic Polynesian food and drink) and it is popular with

The low-rise Hampton Court Hotel

The Harbour Castle Westin, 'the downtown resort on the lake'

travelling business types and legal eagles from the nearby law court. Expensive.

Holiday Inn Downtown, 89 Chestnut Street (tel: 977-0707). Behind City Hall and steps from Chinatown. Indoor and outdoor pools and other big city facilities in the usual moderate Holiday Inn manner. It has 715 rooms and a very popular dining room. Moderately priced.
(There are five other Holiday Inns in Toronto including one near the airport plus one in Oakville and one in Brampton. The central reservations telephone number for all of them is 486-6400.)

Hotel Admiral, 249 Queen's Quay West (tel: 364-5444). This small, recently opened hotel is well placed for the activities of Harbourfront. Great harbour views from its upper outdoor pool area and its 157 rooms are very well appointed. Moderate to expensive.

Hotel Victoria, 56 Yonge Street (tel: 363-1666). Within easy walking distance of the O'Keefe Centre and the St Lawrence Centre, this hotel has been completely renovated and improved. Rooms are small and there are only 42 of them. Good dining room and two cosy and comfortable lounges. Very good value for money. Moderately priced.

The King Edward Hotel, 37 King Street East (tel: 863-9700). A hotel in the grand manner and a landmark since 1900. With all its renovated glories, the 318-room hotel, set in the financial and theatre district, is truly deluxe. Chiaro's is one of the best hotel dining rooms in the city and Sunday brunch at its Café Victoria is an event (see Food

and Drink section page 61).
Very expensive.
L'Hotel, 225 Front Street West
(tel: 597-1400). Adjoining the
Metro Toronto Convention
Centre, its 600 rooms are an
obvious draw for visiting
conventioneers and crowds are
a matter of course. Close to Roy
Thomson Hall and the Royal
Alexandra Theatre, it has a
full-service recreation club
which includes two squash
courts. Wonderful suites (even if
some of them do overlook the
railroad tracks). Expensive.
Novotel Toronto Centre, 45 The
Esplanade (tel: 367-8900).
Recently opened with 266
rooms, it is right behind O'Keefe
Centre, a short walk from the St
Lawrence Market. Its
turn-of-the-century architecture
complements many of the
surrounding buildings.
Moderately priced.

L'Hotel's Skylight Lounge

The Primrose Hotel

Primrose Hotel, 111 Carlton Street (tel: 977-8000). Close to business centres, shopping and entertainment areas, this 334-room hotel has an outdoor swimming pool. Moderate to expensive.

Quality Inn Essex Park Hotel, 300 Jarvis Street (tel: 977-4823). A former apartment building converted to a 96-room hotel, 15 of which are efficiency units, handy if you plan a long-term visit. Inexpensive.

Royal York Hotel, 100 Front Street West (tel: 368-2511). The best known hotel in Toronto, it stands across Front Street from Union Station at the south end of the underground city. It has 1,600 rooms, many restaurants and lounges and the Imperial Room nightclub. (It also has Louis Janetta, the legendary *maitre d'* who knows everyone worth knowing in Toronto and without whom the hotel would probably fall apart.) Expensive. **The Sheraton Centre,** 123 Queen Street West (tel: 361-1000). The underground city also runs through this massive hostelry and it has, as well, over 60 shops and two cinemas on its property. A centre for business meetings and seminars of all kinds, its recreational facilities include an indoor and an outdoor pool. Well located, across from City Hall, its 1,427 rooms and public areas are always busy. Expensive.

Midtown
The Bradgate Arms, 54 Foxbar Road, Avenue Road and St Clair area (tel: 968-1331). Close to the shops and restaurants of the Yonge and St Clair neighbourhood, this small (109 rooms) and charming European-style hotel is also handy for the mansions of exclusive Forest Hill. Getting down to the Avenue Road/Yorkville/Bloor Street shops and the Royal Ontario Museum is also easy. Comfortable bar and very good dining room. Moderately priced.

ACCOMMODATION

The Brownstone Hotel, 15 Charles Street East (tel: 924-7381). Another small hotel with 109 rooms, one block south of Bloor Street just off Yonge Street. It is the sort of hotel you can find in Manhattan — if you are a native or have connections — with a good dining room, a piano bar and a patio which operates May to September. This one is a real find. Moderately priced.

Carlton Inn, near Yonge Street

Carlton Inn Hotel, 30 Carlton Street (tel: 977-6655). Nothing fancy, this is an economy hotel close to Maple Leaf Gardens and Yonge Street, with 536 rooms, a restaurant and two bars. There is also a special money-saving plan called Seniors Service for those aged 60 and over. (The plan also applies to the Chestnut Park Hotel and the Carlton Place Hotel.) Inexpensive.

Four Seasons Hotel, 21 Avenue Road (tel: 964-0411). Set in the midst of fashionable Yorkville, the luxurious touches that are a byword with Four Seasons are everywhere in this 379-room hotel. First-class dining at Truffles and two always-popular bars. Only one criticism: as happens at the Harbour Castle Westin, guests are unfortunately asked to compete with cars at the main entrance. Very expensive.

Loews Westbury Hotel, 475 Yonge Street (tel: 924-0611). Handy for Maple Leaf Gardens, it is not a glamorous hotel but its 540 rooms are comfortable and its restaurant, Creighton's, always dependable. Moderately priced.

Park Plaza Hotel, 4 Avenue Road (tel: 924-5471). This stylish old hotel has recently changed owners and multi-million dollar renovations have been under way on its south tower, with a completion date of November 1989. Meanwhile it is business as usual at the north tower, which fronts Prince Arthur Avenue and where all its restaurants and lounges are located. Though, to the despair of many long-time patrons (especially writers), the Roof Garden bar is temporarily closed, too. Expensive.

Ramada Renaissance Plaza (formerly Hotel Plaza II), 90 Bloor Street East (tel: 961-8000). It is actually six floors of a large apartment building and connected with The Bay department store on Bloor Street, just east of Yonge. With 256 rooms and a private health

Movie star favourite, Sutton Place

club for its guests, it is supremely well situated for midtown attractions. Its Greenery dining room is justifiably popular. Expensive.

Sutton Place Hotel, 955 Bay Street (tel: 924-9221). The financial district and Queen's Park are on the doorstep of this truly luxurious 280-room hotel. Grand European-style service here and it is a favourite haunt of visiting movie stars. The Sanssouci dining room is famed for its décor almost as much as its food. Expensive.

Town Inn, 620 Church Street (tel: 964-3311). Another good bet for long-term visitors, the Town's well-priced accommodation includes mini-suites with fully equipped kitchenettes. As well, there is a sauna, indoor pool and tennis court. Inexpensive.

Windsor Arms Hotel, 22 St Thomas Street (tel: 979-2341). Looking more like an ivy-covered English mansion, this intimate little hotel is an oasis of calm, only steps away from Bloor Street. With only 81 rooms, furnished with antiques, and afternoon tea in the Fireside Lounge, it is a favourite of those who like old-fashioned comfort and very personal service. This is home to The Restaurant and the Courtyard Café and a member of the Relais et Chateaux group. Surprisingly modest rates for some of its rooms, otherwise expensive.

ACCOMMODATION

Inn on the Park: wintersports are on offer in the park in season

North Central
Novotel Hotel-North York, 3 Park Home Avenue, North York (tel: 733-2929). Just west of the northern reaches of Yonge Street and close to Highway 401, it is a well-run, comfortable hotel of 262 rooms, with pool and exercise room, restaurant and bar. Moderately priced.
Roehampton Hotel, 808 Mount Pleasant Road (tel: 487-5101). Close to the excellent little shops of Mount Pleasant and the nightlife of nearby Eglinton Avenue, this small residential hotel has an outdoor pool and discounts for senior citizens. Inexpensive.

East
Four Seasons Inn on the Park, 1100 Eglinton Avenue East (tel: 444-2561). The only resort hotel in the city, it sits on 17 acres (6.9 hectares) next to a 500-acre (200-hectare) park. With three year-round tennis courts, five squash and racketball courts and everything from shuffleboard to cross-country skiing (in season), guests are unlikely to be bored. All-day supervised activities for children. Close to the Ontario Science Centre and what should be easy access to downtown via the Don Valley Parkway. (There are less direct but ultimately faster routes than what is often — because of its susceptibility to traffic jams — termed the Don Valley parking lot.) Good restaurants. Expensive.
Holiday Inn-Don Valley and **Holiday Inn-Scarborough.** Central reservations: tel: 486-6400. Moderately priced.

Howard Johnson Toronto East Hotel, 40 Progress Court, Scarborough (tel: 439-6200). A 24-hour restaurant and mini arcade in this 192-room hotel, with indoor pool and exercise room plus restaurants and lounges. Moderately priced.
The Prince Hotel, 900 York Mills Road (tel: 444-2511). With 15 acres (6 hectares) of parkland, three tennis courts and a complete health club, this large (406 rooms) hotel also boasts the most beautiful Japanese restaurant in the city (see **Katsura,** Food and Drink section page 69.) Other good restaurants and lounges, too. Expensive.
Ramada Hotel-Don Valley, 185 Yorkland Boulevard, Willowdale (tel: 493-9000). All the usual Ramada facilities with 285 rooms, an indoor pool, patio barbecue and a rose garden. Moderately priced.
Sheraton Toronto East Hotel & Towers, (formerly known as the Ramada Renaissance), 2035 Kennedy Road, Scarborough (tel: 229-1500). Handy for visiting the Metro Toronto Zoo, this hotel has a tropical feeling with an atrium rising over its swimming pool, a great draw in the depths of winter. As well, there is squash and racketball, a putting green, sauna and exercise room. A good bet if you are travelling with children. Several restaurants, of which **Santara** (Japanese) is the prettiest. Moderately priced.

West
Holiday Inn-Etobicoke, Central Reservations tel: 486-6400. Moderately priced.

Valhalla Inn, 1 Valhalla Inn Road (tel: 239-2391). Situated midway between Lester B Pearson airport and downtown. Its 250 rooms overlook a garden courtyard and there are three restaurants, three bars and a lounge for dinner dancing. Recreational facilities close by and limousine service to and from the airport. Convenient if you need to stay in the west end of Metro. Moderately priced.

Airport Environs
Airport and Dixon Roads (known as the Airport strip) are lined with hotels, large and small. Most, if not all, run shuttle buses to and from the airport and in the following selection these are either free or at a minimal cost of from $1 to $2 per person. Accommodation costs can vary but can be easily checked via the courtesy hotel telephones at the Arrivals level of the airport terminals.
The Bristol Place Hotel, 950 Dixon Road (tel: 675-9444).
Cara Inn, 6257 Airport Road (tel: 678-1400).
Constellation Hotel, 900 Dixon Road (tel: 675-1500).
Hilton International-Toronto Airport, 5875 Airport Road (tel: 677-9900).
Holiday Inn-Toronto Airport, 970 Dixon Road (tel: 675-7611 or Central Reservations: 486-6400).
Skyline Toronto Airport, 655 Dixon Road (tel: 244-1711).
Toronto Airport Marriott Hotel, 901 Dixon Road (tel: 674-9400).

For Youth Hostel accommodation see Directory, Student and Youth Travel, page 123.

CULTURE, ENTERTAINMENT, NIGHTLIFE

Whether you go for Swan Lake or tap, Sondheim or Neil Simon, Dixieland or Vivaldi your tastes can find an outlet in Toronto. If sports are what turn you on you can spectate or participate, according to the season, to your heart's content and although it is not a 24-hour place for nightlife, Toronto can keep you going till the wee small hours.

In the lounges, bars and nightclubs of the city you can hear every kind of music from rhythm and blues to reggae. You can dress up for a glamorous evening of dining and dancing, try a bit of foot stomping, country-style, ogle a belly-dancer or mingle with the trendy crowd at an after-hours club. The possibilities are limitless, depending only upon your tastes, stamina and willingness to spend.

You can dance at Sparkles, the world's highest nightclub and bar, atop the CN Tower; put on your best and carry your memories of the big bands to the Imperial Room at the Royal York. Or you can elbow your way through the crush at Albert's Hall in the Brunswick House for rock, country and Dixieland, settle in for the evening with jazz at George's Spaghetti House, journey downtown to the elegant little Café des Copains or uptown for more of the same at the informal Chick n' Deli. The range of theatre runs from traditional fare, in plush surroundings, to contemporary and experimental

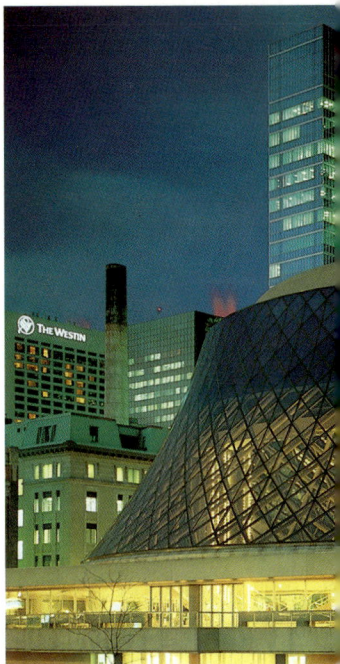

theatre where patrons perch on hard-backed chairs or benches. You can see cabaret or a satirical review, get involved (from the audience) in solving a murder mystery, critique the performance of stand-up comedians in what they hope will be the first step on the road to stardom, or take in opera and ballet at the O'Keefe Centre and a symphony concert at Roy Thomson Hall. On a long visit you might try them all.

There are a myriad of bars and lounges, after-hours clubs and places to dance the night away, some of them sophisticated models of restrained elegance, others crowded, pounding mob

Roy Thomson Hall, one of the centres of musical nightlife

scenes that tempt one to invest in hearing aid futures.

The movie houses are as many and as varied as you would expect to find in a major city and although Toronto's restaurants don't all operate on a late-night basis, it is easy enough to find a snack after the show.

In truth, it is a big city and anything you might want is available somewhere. You can amble around the museums, shop for art in the galleries of Yorkville, indulge a passion for antiques and books, take in football, hockey or baseball, enjoy the theatre, anything you can afford you can usually find. Toronto is, surprisingly, the second largest centre for live theatre in North America (New York is tops) and this means the play's the thing (or opera, ballet, concerts, drama, comedy, etc) all over the city.

Where does it all happen? Here are some of the gathering places:

St Lawrence Centre for the Arts, 27 Front Street East (tel: 366-7723). Toronto's civic cultural centre with concerts, plays, films and public forums.

Massey Hall, 178 Victoria Street (tel: 593-4828). A landmark since

The O'Keefe Centre, Toronto's largest theatre

1894 and former home of the Toronto Symphony, this venerable old lady now plays hostess to a variety of performers and events.
O'Keefe Centre, 1 Front Street East (tel: 872-2262). Home of the Canadian Opera Company and the National Ballet of Canada and the setting for Broadway shows and star names.
Roy Thomson Hall, 60 Simcoe Street (tel: 593-4828). The spectacular new home of the Toronto Symphony and the scene for international performances of jazz, comedy, classical music and the like.
Royal Alexandra Theatre, 260 King Street West (tel: 593-4211). An elegant, turn-of-the-century gem staging some of the city's best plays and musicals.
Premiere Dance Theatre, Queen's Quay Terminal (tel: 973-4000). Contemporary and traditional dance in a beautifully

intimate theatre. (Free shuttle bus runs every 15 minutes from Union Station to Queen's Quay Terminal.)

Some Other Notables
Bathurst Street Theatre, 736 Bathurst Street (tel: 588-6800).
Bayview Playhouse, 1605 Bayview Avenue (tel: 481-6191).
Bluma Apel Theatre, St Lawrence Centre, 27 Front Street East (tel: 366-7723).
Centrestage, 27 Front Street East (tel: 366-7723).
Factory Theatre, 125 Bathurst Street (tel: 864-9971).
Leah Posluns Theatre, 4588 Bathurst Street (tel: 630-6752).
Poor Alex Theatre, 296 Brunswick Avenue (tel: 927-8998).
Tarragon Theatre, 30 Bridgman Avenue (tel: 531-1827).

Theatre Passe Muraille, 16 Ryerson Avenue (tel: 363-2416). **Toronto Free Theatre,** 26 Berkeley Street (tel: 368-2856). **Young People's Theatre,** 165 Front Street East (tel: 864-9732).

Comedy

Rivoli, 334 Queen Street West (tel: 596-1908). Revues and comedians.

Second City, The Old Firehall, 110 Lombard Street (tel: 863-1111). Satire and parody.

Yuk-Yuk's, Downtown: 1280 Bay Street. Stand-up comedians and a chance to polish your act at amateur nights. Uptown: 2335 Yonge Street. Mississauga: 300 Dundas Street East. Information on all three: tel: 967-6425.

Dinner Theatre

The Groaning Board, 131 Jarvis Street (tel: 363-0265). It is not live theatre because the bodies are all on screen but you will see award-winning TV commercials from all over the

The Royal Alexandra Theatre,
for red plush grandeur

world. Terrific fun.

Harper's Restaurant, 38 Lombard Street (tel: 863-6223). Comic cabaret and razzle-dazzle magic.

His Majesty's Feast, Inn on the Lake, 1926 Lakeshore Boulevard West (tel: 769-1165). Medieval hijinks with Henry VIII and a lunatic court.

Limelight Dinner Theatre, 2026 Yonge Street (tel: 482-5200). Scaled-down versions of hit Broadway shows.

Savoy Restaurant, First Canadian Place, Adelaide Street West at Bay Street (tel: 368-2761). Murder mystery evenings.

You can frequently buy half-price tickets for productions at the major theatres on the day of performance from Five Star Tickets, which shares a booth outside The Eaton Centre at Dundas and Yonge Streets with the Metro Visitors Association. Tickets for Stratford and the Niagara-on-the-Lake Shaw Festival can often be bought

there, too, on the day before the performance. Open: Mon to Sat noon to 19.30; Sunday 11.00 to 15.00. (Best bet for theatre, entertainment and nightlife listings and information: the three Toronto newspapers, *The Toronto Star*, the *Globe & Mail* and the *Toronto Sun,* with special emphasis on *The Star's* Friday 'What's On' section; the free tabloid *Now,* a very comprehensive entertainment guide found on news-stands and in restaurants all over the city, and the monthly listings in *Toronto Life* magazine.)

A few places to join the night-time glitterati: **Brandy's** on the Esplanade, across from the Novotel, is packed at lunchtime and even more so in the evening when the dancing begins. It is one of the most consistently popular spots in the area and it connects with neighbouring Scotland Yard (pub food and more music with a lot of regulars).

Over at **Pat & Marios,** at the corner of Wellington and Church Streets, the singles are out in force and at weekends they are lined up outside, champing at the bit to get on to the dance floor.

As the well-heeled shoppers of Yorkville make for home they are replaced with up-and-comers who favour watering holes such as **Hemingway's** and **Remy's** (with a patio which accommodates hundreds), and **South Side Charlie's;** serious jazz

lovers who hang out at **Meyer's;** and those who want to — really want to — see and be seen at the **Bellair,** where there are two levels of dancing and a bar scene which never stops.

Dance, too, at the **Copa,** with its video screens and lasers (would you believe it can hold close to 2,000 people?) and then wander over to the **'22',** at 22 St Thomas Street, in the Windsor Arms, for a quiet drink in what can only be termed more gracious surroundings.

Move uptown to **Berlin** for rhythm and blues but don't be too casual about it. Berlin likes to advise its customers to dress

The Limelight (and many other spots) for informal dinner theatre

elegantly and, judging by the crowds, the customers do not mind at all.

Close by are the two most popular singles' bars in the area, **Earl's Tin Palace** and **Friday's,** always packed and queues at weekends. (No jeans or running shoes at Earl's, please.) Down on Queen Street West is the **BamBoo,** serving up a mixed bag of musical acts that run the gamut from country blues to rock and reggae. Good Caribbean food and owners who know their stuff.

In the East end there are, among others, the dining/ drinking/dancing spots such as **Panama Joe's** and **Spectrum,** as well as several popular pubs such as the **Balmy Arms.**

At the **Amsterdam** (sister to the **Rotterdam**) you can indulge a passion for beer and watch it being brewed, too. It will have to be a noisy passion, mind you, because the bar area is huge and the outdoor seating area a magnet for summer crowds. Pubs such as the **Madison,** the **Balmy Arms** and the **Jack Russell** probably come closest to an authentic British pub, although there are many others scattered through the city and a game of darts can be taken just as seriously here as any place in Britain.

Three places in Toronto consistently recommended by locals should not be missed — the **Chick n' Deli** on Mount Pleasant for great jazz; the **Bluenote** on Pears Avenue for what many agree is the best rhythm and blues, and **El Mocambo** on Spadina Avenue for rock.

Brandy's, popular with locals

A Quick Reference Guide to Night Spots:

Albert's Hall, Brunswick House, 481 Bloor Street West (tel: 964-2242).

Amsterdam, 133 John Street (tel: 595-8201).

Balmy Arms, 2136 Queen Street East (tel: 691-8253).

BamBoo, 312 Queen Street West (tel: 593-5771).

Bellair Café, 100 Cumberland Street (tel: 964-2222).

Berlin, 2335 Yonge Street (tel: 489-7777).

Brandy's, 58 The Esplanade (tel: 364-6671 or 364-6674).

Café des Copains, 48 Wellington Street East (tel: 869-0148).

Chick n' Deli, 744 Mount Pleasant Road (tel: 489-3363).

Club Bluenote, 128 Pears Avenue (tel: 924 8244).

Copa, 21 Scollard Street (tel: 922-6500).

Earl's Tin Palace, 150 Eglinton Avenue East (tel: 487-9281).

El Mocambo, 464 Spadina Avenue (tel: 925-4830).

George's Spaghetti House, 290 Dundas Street East (tel: 923-9887).

Hemingway's, 142 Cumberland Street (tel: 968-2828).

Imperial Room, Royal York Hotel, 100 Front Street West (tel: 368-2511 or 368-6175).

The Madison, 14 Madison Avenue (tel: 927-1722).

Meyer's Deli, 69 Yorkville Avenue (tel: 960-4780).

Panama Joe's, 124 Danforth Avenue (tel: 463-0085).

Pat & Mario's, 35 Church Street (tel: 366-7800). Uptown at 2300 Yonge Street (tel: 485-7999).

Pimblett's, 263 Gerrard Street East (tel: 929-9525).

Remy's, 115 Yorkville Avenue (tel: 968-9429).

The Jack Russell, 27 Wellesley Street East (tel: 967-9442).

South Side Charlie's, 121 Yorkville Avenue (tel: 929-0316).

Sparkles, CN Tower, 301 Front Street West (tel: 597-8138).

Spectrum, 2714 Danforth Avenue (tel: 699-9913).

22, at the Windsor Arms Hotel, 22 St Thomas Street (tel: 979-2341).

WEATHER AND WHEN TO GO

Toronto has a pretty nice climate, all in all, though the average first frost does come on 29 October and the average last frost doesn't melt away until the dawn of 21 April. In between those dates it can get really frigid, but usually not in any sustained way. In fact, the presence of Lake Ontario keeps the Toronto area relatively warm compared with nearby points in Ontario, and the direction of the prevailing wind dumps the bulk of the winter's snow on poor old Buffalo, NY, to the south of the lake.

Not that Toronto gets no snow. Visitors coming between early December and late March should carry clothing — sweaters, overcoats, scarves — that can be worn in layers and will keep them warm at freezing temperatures. The clothing may not be needed every day but a little extra baggage weight is better than turning blue in an Arctic blast.

Have rubber or plastic outer footwear, too, or waterproof boots, because road gangs in Canada throw enough salt to create the Dead Sea at every corner and the saline solution that results is almost as corrosive on leather as it is on ice. And there does not have to be a heavy snowfall to bring out the salt trucks, just frost conditions and water on the roads.

Average temperatures in January and February run just under freezing and in March daytime averages move above that point, but none of that means there will not be a blizzard or a cold snap, which is not all that bad if you are wearing layered clothing and are prepared for it.

To step outside when the air is like chilled wine and the snow crackles under your feet is to feel an aliveness no southern clime can impart. Or so Canadians keep telling themselves.

Summer average temperatures are moderate, too, but averages only reveal the middle range. The reality is that in July or August visitors can expect at least some days that are well into the 90sF (high 30sC) with a humidity near the top of the scale. Book air-conditioned accommodation with or near a swimming pool and rent cars with air conditioning. Then relax and enjoy the heat, as Canadians do, with a retreat conveniently at hand.

Take the lightest summer clothing you own plus a light

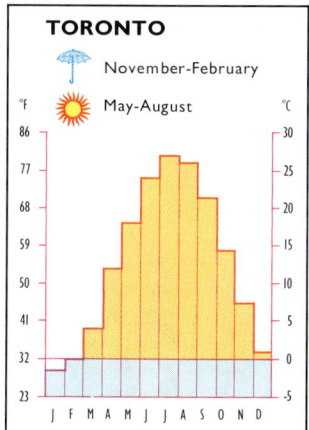

TORONTO

November-February

May-August

| | J | F | M | A | M | J | J | A | S | O | N | D |

jacket or top to deal with the chills of air-conditioning. And while shorts and brief sundresses are fine for Harbourfront and the Islands, they are rare elsewhere.

Men will need jacket and tie in the better restaurants, winter or summer, and women a dress or dressy trousers.

Unless it is a really gala event there will not be much in the way of formal evening gowns and dinner jackets in Toronto. All in all, big-city wear is much the same now the world over and the city has more than its fair share of designer jeans.

HOW TO BE A LOCAL

In spring, summer and early fall that involves getting caught up in Blue Jay fever, being a fan, talking incessantly about Blue Jays and joining the crowd at the city's new SkyDome for home games. And, if you really want to fit in, wear one of those long-visored Blue Jay baseball caps that make you look like Admiral Nimitz. Or Daffy Duck. But when Toronto empties on Friday evenings in the summer forget the games and join the exodus to cottage country in Muskoka north of the city, to enjoy the pleasure of woodland and lake. Travel Ontario at 965-4008 can give you a list of the resorts.

Less expensive ways of melting into the crowd include relaxing at Harbourfront or Ontario Place in the summer, picnicking on Toronto Islands and canoeing the lagoons, visiting St Lawrence Market on Saturday mornings for coffee any time of the year and skating on the reflecting pool in Nathan Phillips Square in winter.

Caribana: the Caribbean festival starts with a parade

SPECIAL EVENTS

Every year new events crowd the calendar, then disappear, but there are some that stand steady down the years — festivals and celebrations that have caught the hearts or the minds of the public and are welcomed back like old friends when their season rolls around. Such are the following:

Canadian National Exhibition

The oldest and largest annual exhibition in the world, the Ex is held annually in the last two weeks in August and the long Labour Day weekend and is, in effect, a traditional country fair grown gigantic. Just like those small-town autumn celebrations it has hot dogs and booths and the old army game (betting on the spin of a wheel) and prize cows and dog shows and baseball games. But its attractions also include one of the world's great air shows (on the Labour Day weekend), exhibits from other nations and a grandstand show that features Hollywood and Las Vegas entertainment — or such spectacular performers as the massed bands of the Highland regiments. It is strictly Big Time on the entertainment circuit, despite the hoopla, thrill rides and bingo barkers. It makes for a great day in the outdoors — but it attracts hundreds of thousands of people so you have to like crowds.

Caribana

This wild week of Caribbean reggae, food, limbo dancing and mirth begins with a shimmering, strutting parade down University Avenue and a ferry ride to Centre Island for steel band concerts, floating nightclubs and gyrating celebrants. Stage areas on the island throb with loud music and spectacular dancing, impromptu outbursts of exuberance and swirling colour. And while all this goes on the crowds keep coming until the island is crammed with costumed revellers. Labour Day week, September. For information call 925-5435.

Festival of Festivals

This celebration of world cinema starts on the first Thursday after Labour Day and runs for 10 days. The films play at downtown cinemas and apart from avid fans the Festival attracts a horde of international movie makers, buyers and critics, not to mention some of the stars themselves. During this period the élite meet at all the best places and the entertainment pages of the morning newspapers are crammed with who was seen where, doing what, with whom. In other words, it is a major event, as testified by this comment from a *New York Times* film critic: 'Studios now consider this festival the main testing ground for new films.' The Festival of Festivals' box office opens in mid-July. Call 968-FILM for all information.

Metro International Caravan

A nine-day festival with more than 50 pavilions scattered about the city offering food, drink, crafts and entertainment from countries around the world. Held in the second half of June, it is an ethnic celebration run by the local representatives of each culture, with churches, community halls and clubs serving as temporary pavilions and it is as authentic as a trip back home.

Entertainment is as wide as the world — dance groups, choirs, floor shows, musical theatre, jazz, folk songs, gymnasts — and entrance is by Caravan passport, obtainable at any pavilion. Special buses travel from pavilion to pavilion but you will never make it to more than two or three in an evening without bursting or toppling over from strong drink. For information call 977-0466.

The Molson Indy series races take place on the city streets

Molson Indy

The premier open wheel racing series in North America, the CART/PPG Indy Car World Series, comes to Toronto every mid-July with weekend races on the city streets around the Canadian National Exhibition grounds. The world series is a run of 15 events, including the Indy 500 and the Toronto races, which take place in cities all over North America for the National Championship. The powerful cars are not all that different from Formula One cars, though they have retained the turbo engines which have now been banned in Formula One vehicles. For ticket information call 595-5445.

Player's International/Player's Challenge

Canada's top tennis tournament is played at the National Tennis Centre on the campus of York University for the one week in late August directly preceding the US Open.

Toronto's different ethnic backgrounds join in the annual Metro International Caravan. Above, a Chinese lion dance

It is actually a two-city, Toronto and Montréal, affair, with the men's event, the Player's International, and the women's event, the Player's Challenge, alternating cities each year. The hard court tournament attracts many of the world's top-ranked international players. For information call 665-9777.

Royal Agricultural Winter Fair

Every autumn Toronto gets back to its roots with this 10-day winter fair, a far more dignified — and top drawer — event than the Canadian National Exhibition. It is the largest of its

kind in the world, attracting competitors and spectators from as far away as Japan to ogle everything from giant Clydesdales to rutabagas (swedes). The best in horses, cattle and farm produce are on exhibit and a highlight is the Royal Horse Show, which draws jumping teams from the wide world.

The time is mid-November and the setting is the Coliseum at Exhibition Place. For information call 393-6401.

CHILDREN

Toronto offers a whole world of entertainment for children, ranging from museums, hockey, skating and skiing in winter to watery pursuits in the heat of summer, but the following have been chosen with an eye to providing parents with some entertainment, too. For that reason some items duplicate, in part, listings in other sections of this book.

BLACK CREEK PIONEER VILLAGE

Jane Street and Steeles Avenue
Pigs, cows, horses and sheep, wagons and sleighs, farm buildings and 19th-century toys are all spread out for the delight of youngsters who head back to pioneer times at this restored village. In winter there is skating, cross-country and horse-drawn sleigh rides, in summer there is the blacksmith and farm hands to watch, all dressed in the costumes of the day. For information call 736-1733 or (a 24-hour tape) 661-6610.

Canada's Wonderland — a theme park paradise for children

CANADA'S WONDERLAND

Commercial, noisy, expensive and crowded but tops on any youngster's hit parade with a centrepiece man-made mountain, 33 rides, fast foods, a Salt Water Circus of sealions and dolphins and fantasy lands where children can be photographed with the Flintstones or the Smurfs or other cartoon characters. A day will go quickly and so will your cash. For information call 1-832-2205.

CASA LOMA

1 Austin Terrace
Here is a castle where they can act out their fantasies, with real turrets, a secret staircase and hidden passages just like the ones in all those horror movies, and battlements from which to withstand the foe. It is the answer to every youngster's dream and if you cannot afford to build or buy one, a day tour here is the least you can do. For information call 923-1171.

CENTREVILLE

Centre Island
A pint-sized children's amusement park modelled on a turn-of-the-century village, with 15 inexpensive rides, games, arcades, miniature golf and a small petting zoo. And all with the bonus of a ferry ride over to the island and back.

CHILDREN'S BOOK STORE

604 Markham Street
A treasure trove of books for the younger set, all the classics you remember and the new ones, too. And on Sundays in the spring and autumn there are often readings or concerts. Open seven days a week. For details call 535-7011.

HARBOURFRONT

Queen's Quay
Full of activities of all sorts to please young people.
Kaleidoscope, Saturdays and Sundays and some holidays from 11.30 to 16.00, offers youngsters and their parents a chance to work together at arts and crafts, finger painting, doll making, basket weaving. There is no charge and you can take your work of art home. Then there is: **Kids' Stage** throughout the summer with outdoor performances by mimes, puppeteers, singers and performers of all kinds; **Summer Fun,** daily arts, craft and music demonstrations in which children can get involved; and, in May, a week of appearances by performers from around the world at the **Milk International Children's Festival.** For information on these and other activities call 973-3000.

HIGH PARK

Queen Street West
It takes a little bread (literally) for children to have a ball feeding the geese, ducks, swans and other birds on Grenadier Pond. There are other animals in the park, too, and if you have the foresight to take along some extra bread there are plenty of places for that joy of childhood, a picnic.

KORTRIGHT CENTRE

Kleinburg, Ont
The full name of this 400-acre (160-hectare) nature park is the Kortright Centre for Conservation and it offers everything a young naturalist would find fascinating: nature trails, plant and wildlife studies, bat nights, birdhouse building, maple syrup tours, beekeeping, wildflower and autumn colour walks, and more. Winter or summer there is always something going on at the centre, which is just one of 13 valley areas controlled by the Metropolitan Toronto and Region Conservation Authority. So if you do not find what you want at Kortright, which is open from 10.00 to 16.00 daily, try one of the others. For information on any of them call 661-6600 between 08.30 to 16.30 Monday to Friday, and 08.00 to 14.30 Saturday and Sunday.

METRO TORONTO ZOO

Meadowvale Road, Scarborough
Any zoo is a fascination for children but this is one of the good ones, with the animals given some space to move about and even, on occasion, privacy. There are camel and pony rides and feeding sessions and young animals to see and, all in all, it could be a long and exhausting day. But they will love it . . . and remember it. Open every day but Christmas from 09.30 with closing at 16.30 in winter, 19.00 in summer. Easiest to reach by car but accessible on public transit with a long bus ride. For information call 392-5900.

ONTARIO PLACE
Exhibition Place
This is a delight on a summer day, with a Children's Village full of innovative play equipment and a play area for the small fry, 12 or under, where water squirts and flows and sprays from everything, even bicycles, and the youngsters scream and love it. The bigger folk, including adults, can opt for the Water Slide, which offers 370

Ontario Place, an amusement park with something for everyone

feet (112m) of slippery slopes and tunnels and a final plunge into a pool. These, along with other attractions such as the Owl Discovery Centre, which presents a 15-minute puppet show telling children about science, put Ontario Place at the top of the wish list for youngsters. For information call 965-7711.

ONTARIO SCIENCE CENTRE
770 Don Mills Road at Eglinton Avenue East
Here is a place where it is hard to decide whether children or

parents are getting the most enjoyment out of the experiments and props. Act for and run video cameras, get charged with electricity, watch bees at work — there are hundreds of things to do, all designed to amuse and entertain, and teach you as well. It gets top rating. Reachable by public transit on a long ride. For information call 429-0193.

THE PUPPET CENTRE
171 Avondale Avenue, North York

This is a museum with 25 exhibits of puppets down the ages and around the world and puppet shows on Saturdays at 15.00. It has a gift shop as well where you can buy hand, rod or finger puppets or marionettes, from the very cheap to the very expensive. The centre is on the lower level of Glen Avon School and there is an admission charge if you attend a puppet performance. For information call 222-9029.

RIVERDALE FARM
Riverdale Park
The site of Toronto's old zoo has been transformed into a real farm where children can visit the 19th century and mingle with farmyard animals, horses, ducks, chickens, cows, goats and such, and pet the little ones. And all right in the heart of the city. There is no fee and the farm is open all year, roughly from 09.00 to 16.00 in winter, 09.00 to 17.00 in summer. For information call 392-6794.

ROYAL ONTARIO MUSEUM
100 Queen's Park
Not everything at this superb museum will interest children but there are things that cannot fail — the totem poles and dinosaurs, for instance, and the Chinese dragons and the bat cave. And if they are six or older they will love the Discovery Gallery where they can actually handle and experiment with ancient artefacts. You may have to hurry through some galleries where you would like to linger but it will be a day to remember. For information call 586-5549.

YOUNG PEOPLE'S THEATRE
165 Front Street East
A professional theatrical company that performs plays for children during a season which runs from September to June. The range of works includes everything from Shakespeare and *Kidnapped* to adaptations of Canadian novels. Performances are usually presented Friday and Saturday evenings, with matinées on Saturdays and Sundays. Audiences range from 6 to 15 years of age and information can be had during the season by calling 864-9732 (the box office) and all year by calling 363-5131 (the main office).

Two all-time favourite restaurants for children are **Ginsberg & Wong,** Village by the Grange, 71 McCaul Street and at 390 Steeles Avenue West, and **The Organ Grinder,** 58 The Esplanade.

Note: The tabloid *Kids' Toronto* is an excellent monthly publication which lists a wide range of activities for children of all ages. Available, free, at the Ontario Science Centre, The Royal Ontario Museum, the Art Gallery of Ontario and at some shops.

Crowds of young people take to their skates when the pool in Nathan Phillips Square ices over

TIGHT BUDGET

With rates under $20 the **Toronto International Youth Hostel** is undoubtedly the least expensive place to stay in Toronto. The local representative of the International Youth Hostel Association, it has no age restrictions and offers 180 beds in dormitories and semi-private rooms. Better yet, it runs the Youth Hostel Travel Agency, which offers reduced-rate tours and even discounts on transportation to the airport and tickets to local attractions. Both the hostel and the agency are at 223 Church Street Toronto, Ont M5B 1Y7, and can be reached

by telephone at 368-0207. The reception desk is open from 08.30 to 23.00.

The University of Toronto has 750 campus rooms available between 24 May and 27 August. There is a small fee for the use of athletic complex facilities and parking is available (tel: 978-8735).

There are a number of Bed and Breakfast places in Metro. Find out about them through:

Downtown Toronto Association of Bed and Breakfast Guest Homes, tel: 598-4562 or 977-6841.

The Association represents 25 single and double occupancy rooms in centrally located, restored Victorian-era homes in some of the city's most interesting neighbourhoods. The best time to call the main number is between 09.30 and noon.

Metropolitan Bed and Breakfast Registry of Toronto, tel: 964-2566 or 928-2833.

Some 50 homes are represented, many conveniently located for easy access to downtown attractions.

The least expensive way to get around the city, using the Toronto Transit Commission trams, buses and subways, is in most cases the best way. For detailed information pick up a free Ride Guide at subway entrances or call 393-INFO from 07.00 to 23.30 daily.

Half-price theatre tickets for the day of performance are available from the Five Star Ticket kiosk outside the Eaton Centre at Yonge and Dundas Streets.

DIRECTORY

Arriving

By Air Toronto's Pearson (International) Airport has two terminals, with a third under construction, but like many major airports around the world it is crowded, in the air and on the ground. Air Canada, British Airways and a number of other national carriers use Terminal Two, a long, rectangular building on two levels, while Canadian Airlines International, Wardair and several other scheduled airlines and charters use Terminal One, an older circular building which tends to jam up with passengers and relatives at busy flight times. Customs and immigration clearances are necessary for passengers arriving in Canada from other countries but though there are queues they move fairly quickly. British citizens need passports, but not normally visas; US citizens need only proof of citizenship such as a birth certificate, though obviously a passport would prove that too. Citizens of some other countries need visas, others do not. Check before setting off.

There are no currency restrictions but there are limits on duty-free liquor (40 ounces) and cigarettes (200). Also there are strict controls on agricultural materials, fruits, vegetables, meats and plants and on any product using any part of an animal belonging to any

Toronto's Pearson International Airport, just as crowded as many another major airport

endangered species.

There are porters available in the baggage claim area (tip about $1 per bag) but there are also free baggage carts. If there are none there when you arrive wait a few moments. They are constantly being collected and returned.

Just outside the Arrivals level at both terminals are bus stops for coaches that travel to hotels in downtown Toronto, about 20 miles (32km) away, or connect with the Toronto Transit Commission (TTC) subways. The TTC bus (No 58A) travels from Terminal Two only to the Lawrence West subway station. One Gray Coach bus goes to the York Mills and Yorkdale subway stations, a second goes to Islington subway station and the third goes to downtown hotels.

Airport area hotels have shuttle buses (you will find hotel ads and telephone numbers on the Arrivals level) and there are taxi ranks and limousines, where at busy periods customers queue up for transport. Fares to the city on both run in the $20 to $30 range, depending on distance and traffic — it is a matter of personal choice, but if you want a limousine don't be fobbed off with a taxi, particularly if you are not headed for downtown Toronto, where most cabbies want to go. For trips into remote or rural areas limousines are a far better bet so make sure which queue you are joining. (Transport Canada's centres at the airport, incidentally, can be reached by calling (416) 676-3506 for information on the airport, flights and tourist attractions. For the names and routes of all carriers out of Toronto contact Aeronautical Information Services, Transport Canada, Ottawa, Ont K1A 0N8, or telephone (613) 995-0197.)

By rail Toronto is served by VIA Rail, which handles most passenger train traffic in the country, with some services from Amtrak, the US public rail carrier, and the Ontario Northland Railway, which runs trains as far north as Moosonee on James Bay. All carry passengers into majestic old Union Station on Front Street across from the Royal York Hotel and within a block of Yonge Street deep in the heart of downtown Toronto. Union is the hub of the subway's system, too, and the terminal for the local GO (Government of Ontario) commuter rail system and it has a taxi rank at the front so there is no problem finding local transportation. VIA Rail, which is the agent for Amtrak and for the Ontario Northland, can be reached on 366-8411, Amtrak itself is toll-free on 1-800-426-8725. GO Transit can be reached on 665-0022.

By bus Out of town buses arrive and depart from the Bus Terminal at 610 Bay Street, just north of Dundas Street. Fares and schedules for all the bus companies can be obtained by calling 393-7911.

Camping

There are no campgrounds within Metro Toronto but a number are within easy reach by car. Among the closer ones are:

Double-decker trains wait in the sidings. Union Station is in the heart of downtown Toronto

Cedar Beach Park at Musselman's Lake, Stouffville, Ont L4A 7X3; open mid-May to mid-October; 535 sites, a picnic park, beach, pools, restaurant and, of all things, a ballroom. Tel: 1-640-1525 or 1-640-1700.

Glen Rouge Campground, 1 Eastville Avenue, Scarborough, Ont M1M 2N5; showers, beach near by, playground, near public transit. Tel: (416) 392-2541 or 392-8092.

Milton Heights Campground, RR 3, Milton, Ont L9T 2X7; 450 sites, huge pool with solar heating, recreation hall, showers, games room. Tel: 1-878-6781.

Toronto West KOA Kampground, PO Box 198.

Campbellville, Ont L0P 1B0; 100 sites, playground, recreational room, pool, laundry, groceries, TV room, showers, fire places. Tel: 1-854-2495.

For information on other campgrounds call Ontario Travel at 965-4008 or the toll-free number for most of Canada and the US outside the city, 1-800-268-3735. Or write ahead for the booklet called *Camping* to Ontario Travel, Queen's Park, Toronto, Ont M7A 2E5.

Car Breakdown
Pull over to the side of the road, if possible, and put up the hood (bonnet) of your car as a signal of distress. Police will stop and help you get to a phone or radio for you and fellow drivers may well stop to help. Car rental companies will replace vehicles if there is a breakdown and there are a number of firms providing towing and emergency road service, all of them listed in the Yellow Pages under Towing. If you are an AAA, AA, AIT or RAC member the Canadian Automobile Association Toronto, 2 Carlton Street, will provide club services. The number for road emergencies is 966-3000.

Car Hire
Renting a car in Canada can be quick and easy. You must be 25 years of age, produce identification and a valid national or international driver's licence and be able to pay, whether with cash, travellers' cheques or credit cards. All the major international car rental companies are represented in Toronto, along with Tilden, a major Canadian company. You will find them listed in the Toronto telephone directory Yellow Pages under Automobile Rental, but meanwhile, some numbers: Tilden, 922-2600; Hertz, 620-9600; Budget, 673-3322 or 676-1240; Thrifty, 868-0350; Avis, 622-9905.

Chauffeur Driven Cars
Toronto's status as a prime movie location may have something to do with the Hollywood-like profusion of posh vehicles available. Want a bar, a VCR, a TV or a cellular phone back there with you? No problem. Everything but a wine cellar is available in the cars parading through the more than 13 pages of listings for luxury chauffeured automobiles in the Yellow Pages, anything from an

antique Rolls-Royce to the newest and shiniest of stretched Cadillacs. Just look under Limousine and have your credit card ready.

Chemist
See **Pharmacist**

Crime
Toronto has little crime for its size, at least by North American standards, but it is a big city and growing, so the possibility is always present. You can walk the downtown streets at night in safety, as residents claim, but as in any big city it is wise to use discretion. Do not take short-cuts through dark alleys or linger on deserted industrial streets. Use common sense and if, despite that, you are robbed or assaulted or injured in any way phone the Metro emergency number, 911, immediately. Any pay phone will accept your call without coins and policemen, ambulance attendants, firemen,

whoever you need, will be sent to the scene. If you want to contact police in a non-emergency situation phone 324-2222.

Customs
There are no restrictions of currency or on most personal possessions but there are limits on duty-free liquor (40 ounces) and cigarettes (200). Also there are strict controls on agricultural materials, fruits, vegetables, meats and plants and on any product using any part of an animal belonging to an endangered species.

Domestic Travel
Public transport in and around Metro is provided by four basic transportation authorities: The Toronto Transit Commission (TTC) which runs the streetcar, bus and subway systems within

Getting around: by taxi, on the buses — which cover the whole city . . .

. . . or by streetcar. The system is efficient, inexpensive and easy to follow

the community; Metro Parks Department, which operates the ferries to Toronto Islands; Gray Coach Lines, which supplies services to nearby communities and offers tours and coach trips; and GO Transit (with the initials standing for Government of Ontario), which operates commuter trains and buses to communities outside the Metro boundaries. The TTC is by far the largest operation and the one visitors encounter most frequently.

Subway TTC's best-known operation, the subway describes a huge narrow U through the city with the Bloor/Danforth line forming a cross stroke. One arm of the U starts at Finch Avenue in the north and runs south under Yonge Street before making a slow turn west through Union Station and travelling north again under University Avenue and Spadina Avenue to Wilson Avenue in the northwest. The Bloor/Danforth line runs from Kipling Avenue in the west to Kennedy Road in the east, with the Scarborough Rapid Transit Line extending the service north and east at ground level to Scarborough City Centre.

The subway system runs from 06.00 to 01.00 Monday to Saturday and from 09.00 to 01.00 on Sunday.

Streetcars, trolley buses and buses Busy downtown routes run a five-minute service during the day with slightly greater intervals between vehicles in the evenings but there can be delays. Surface stops are usually every two blocks and are

DIRECTORY

marked by a red and white sign on utility poles. If you stand by the sign the bus or tram will stop for you. Drivers will be helpful if you are uncertain about your stop, which you may request by tugging on the wire that circles the interior just above the windows.

Trams and buses connect with subways and a single ticket, with transfers (get them when you board your first tram, bus or subway train, not as you leave), will carry you through the whole systém. Tokens (buy them at stations) and tickets are interchangeable and since exact fares are required on streetcars and buses it is a wise idea to buy a few in advance. There are Sunday and holiday passes that allow unlimited travel. For details check the number below.

Tram and bus hours vary, depending on the route, with some providing overnight service, though most do not. For information on any part of the system or to ask for a routing, call 393-INFO.

Since there is a small permanent population on Toronto Islands and some other citizens like to walk the chill lake shores in winter, there is a **ferry** service all year from the city. But hours and frequency change not only with the seasons but with the day of the week, so call the Metro Parks Department on 392-8193 for schedules at the time of your visit. Summer, obviously, is the popular season, with a frequent service, and it is the best time to visit the Islands. But stay away at weekends when there are queues for the ferries and the parks are packed (well, more populated than they are during the week). Do your island tour Monday to Friday.

Gray Coach Operating out of the Bus Terminal at 610 Bay Street, just north of Dundas, this provides services to other nearby Ontario communities and also offers some excellent tours to such places as Niagara Falls and Stratford as well as excursions to celebrations, festivals and such special events as the September/October colour show in the hardwood forests to the north. For information call 393-7911.

Taxis May be telephoned or hailed on the street when the overhead light is on to signify that the cab is vacant (it goes on when the meter is turned back after a fare is paid). Most cabs use standard North American type cars, not special taxi bodies, and have far less room for people, hats or luggage than London cabs (for example) and they have no division between passengers and driver. Nor are drivers, many of whom are newly arrived immigrants without fluency in English, as know-ledgeable about Toronto streets as London cabbies are about their city. So hesitation and use of street directories is common. A proposed regulation to pro-hibit smoking totally in taxis has been the cause of some heated debate. The meter starts at $2 whenever you hire a cab and jumps up by 25 cents every 305 metres (1,000 feet). The three major cab companies in Metro are Co-Op, 364-8161; Diamond, 366-6868; Metro, 363-5611.

*A ferry service operates
year-round to the Toronto Islands*

Driving Driving in Toronto, as in
the United States, is on the right.
There are no roundabouts; huge
X signs at the roadsides mark
crossings where pedestrians
have the right of way; you can
make a right turn on a red light
provided you come to a full stop
first and the way is clear.
Some other things to remember:
all accidents involving personal
injury or property damage over
$700 must be reported to the
police and you are required to
stay at the scene until given
permission to leave (in Metro
call police on 324-2222 and in
rural areas call the Ontario
Provincial Police by dialling 0
and asking the operator for
Zenith 50000); use of seat belts
for all occupants of a car is
mandatory, not just the driver
and front seat passengers;
infants must be strapped in
infant car seats; you must stop
behind the rear door of any

streetcar discharging or picking up passengers unless there is a safety island at the stop; if you drive out of Toronto and encounter a yellow school bus stopped with all its lights flashing you MUST stop whichever direction you are travelling; all distances and speed limits are in kilometres, not miles; gasoline (petrol) is sold by the litre (4.5 to an imperial gallon, 3.8 to a US gallon). The only document necessary is a valid driver's licence, unless you bring your own car, in which case you will need a valid registration or ownership form and proof of insurance. The minimum liability insurance in Ontario is $200,000. Except for the pedestrian cross-walk X sign (which is a Metro device, not province-wide), road signs are those common to the Western world, with a diagonal stroke indicating a prohibition. Be warned, though, that if you drive through the province of Québec you will find one very important difference: stop signs there, unlike those in the rest of the Western world, do not say 'STOP'. They say 'ARRET'. Metro drivers are fast and not overly courteous, with a

A car is a doubtful asset. Use public transport or taxis

tendency to rapid lane changes
and tail-gating (coming up close
to your rear bumper).
The importance of a car within
Metro is dubious. Taxis and
public transit will take you
anywhere you want to go,
parking is high-priced and
sometimes impossible to find
and the stress can be extreme.
If you have a car the best bets
for parking are the publicly
owned Toronto Parking
Authority lots to be found
throughout the city by following
the signs which show an arrow
and a white capital P on a green
background. For information on
lots and rates call 393-7275 or
(at weekends) 393-7300.
If you are driving, and
undoubtedly a car is useful if
you plan out-of-town excursions
to such places as Niagara Falls
and Stratford, then except at
rush hours you will find the
expressways the fastest avenues
out of Toronto. The city itself
was laid out in an east/west,
north/south grid pattern and the
Gardiner Expressway runs east
and west across the south, near
the lakeshore, connecting to the
west with the Queen Elizabeth
Way, which will take you to
Niagara Falls and the US
border.
Across the top of the city
is another east/west
expressway, Highway 401,
which will carry you to Montréal
in the east or Windsor/Detroit
in the west, and squaring off
the pattern are two north/south
highways, the Don Valley
Parkway at the east edge of
the downtown area, and
Highway 427, toward the
western end of Metro.

Driving
See **Domestic Travel**

Electricity
Electrical power is 110 volts, 60
amps, alternating current with
appliances requiring twin-
pronged, flat-tongued plugs.

Embassies, Consulates
Since Toronto is the capital of a
province but not a country there
are no embassies (they can be
reached in Ottawa by dialling
1-613-555-1212 and asking the
operator for the number of the
embassy you seek). However,
Toronto has a number of
consulates easily found in the
white pages telephone
directory under Consulate and
in the consumer section of the
Yellow Pages under Consulates
and Other Foreign Government
Representatives.

**Emergency Telephone
Numbers**
Police, fire and ambulances 911.
You need not use a coin to dial
this number from pay phones.
Poison 598-5900. The number
reaches the Poison Information
Centre, Hospital for Sick
Children.
Child illness 598-5817. The
number reaches the Hospital for
Sick Children's Medical
Information centre, staffed by
specially trained nurses 24
hours a day.
Dental service 967-5649
weekdays, 08.30 to 01.00.
Weekends and holidays,
924-8041, 09.00 to 01.00. The first
number reaches the Academy
of Dentistry and offers a referral
service to dentists, the second
puts you in touch with a dentist.

Optical repairs 364-0740 and 863-6221. The first number is Public Optical, 69 Queen Street East, which offers one-hour service on most optical prescriptions and is open until 21.00 on weekdays and 18.00 on Saturdays. Tel: 638-2998 for Sunday hours. The second number is for United Optical, 27 Queen Street East, which offers same-day service.

Legal help 947-3330. During regular business hours the number reaches the Law Society of Upper Canada at Osgoode Hall, 130 Queen Street West, which offers a free lawyer referral service.

Luggage repairs 598-3469. During regular store hours (which can include evenings) Gold's Luggage Shop will offer repairs while you wait.

Pet problems 464-3501 or 222-5409 for emergency veterinary service. The first number will reach one of several Veterinary Emergency Clinic units, this one at 1180 Danforth Avenue. Telephone numbers of any closer clinic can be obtained there. The clinics deal only with emergencies and are open Monday to Thursday, 19.00 to 08.00, and from 19.00 Fridays to 08.00 Mondays. The second number reaches Willowdale Animal Clinic, 265 Sheppard Avenue West, between Yonge and Bathurst, which is open 24 hours a day and has an animal ambulance. Pets may be brought into Canada provided they have rabies certificates.

Pharmacies open 24 hours a day, 979-2424 or 924-7760/69. The first is for Shopper's Drug Mart, 700 Bay Street at Gerrard Street, the second is for Owl Drug Ltd (formerly Boots), 68 Wellesley Street at Church Street. Also, some pharmacies are open until midnight. Check the Yellow Pages.

Entertainment
The range of entertainment available is as wide as your taste: everything from poetry readings at Harbourfront and ballet at the O'Keefe to wrestling at Maple Leaf Gardens and demolition Derby's at the Canadian National Exhibition grandstand.
You can troll for huge salmon in the waters of the lake in late summer (*The Star* has a fishing contest that pays thousands to winners) or watch the Blue Jays and the Toronto Argonauts in professional baseball and Canadian Football League action at the city's new domed stadium; see the fastest game in the world when the Toronto Maple Leafs play hockey at the Gardens or tee off at Glen Abbey, the course of the Canadian Open in nearby Oakville, or on a score of other courses within easy reach of downtown Toronto.
For information on Blue Jay American League games or for seats write to the club at 300 The Esplanade West, Box 3200, Toronto, Ont M5V 3B3, or telephone (416) 341-1234.
For information on Argonaut Football Club action write to the club at Exhibition Stadium, Toronto, Ont M6K 3C3, or telephone (416) 595-9600.
For information on National League Hockey games write to

the Maple Leafs at 60 Carlton
Street, Toronto, Ont M5B 1L1 or
telephone (416) 977-1641.
If you want to do, not watch, and
tennis is your thing then
telephone 392-7259 to find out
about the free use of City courts.
Or, if you are a racing fan, you
will find two forms of the sport
in Toronto — and neither one is
steeplechase. One is the
traditional flat racing with
thoroughbreds and the other is
harness racing, using
standardbred horses harnessed
to light sulkies. The latter, using
sturdy horses that are less
delicate than thoroughbreds,
was a farm sport that grew into
the big time and now runs all
year at Greenwood racetrack,
Queen Street and Coxwell
Avenue in the heart of the city,
and at Mohawk Raceway just
west of Metro.
Thoroughbred racing takes
place at Greenwood, too, in the

*Join the baseball crowds for a
taste of Blue Jay fever*

spring and autumn, and at
Woodbine track on the city's
northwestern edge from May to
October. It is at Woodbine that
the top race in Canada, the
Queen's Plate, is run early each
July. The third track in the
province, Fort Erie, near
Niagara Falls, has the same
season as Woodbine.
There are two major differences
between British and Ontario
tracks: the horses run
counter-clockwise and
bookmaking is illegal. You can
bet, but only at *pari-mutuels*. For
information on flat racing and
harness racing call the Ontario
Jockey Club on 675-6110.
Then, of course, there is the
Royal Ontario Museum and the
Ontario Science Centre to see
and all those other fascinations
to while away your days. Or, in

summer, you can simply put your feet up and watch the world go by, picnic at Tommy Thompson Park (the Leslie Street Spit) while birdwatching, or on Toronto Islands or at Harbourfront, drift down island lagoons in a canoe or try the giant Water Slide at Ontario Place.

In the evening you can go dining or dancing, or both, or watch live theatre or any one of hundreds of movies, enjoy a cabaret show with your dinner, soak up opera or delight in ballet. Or just go drinking at a topless bar. To each his own. For more details of where to find your heart's desire, pass a pleasant evening or just gratify a whim, see the entertainment section of this guidebook (page 88), but here are some things to know.

You can frequently buy half-price tickets for productions at the major theatres on the day of performance from the Five Star Ticket booth, outside The Eaton Centre at Dundas and Yonge Streets. Open: Monday to Saturday noon to 19.30; Sunday 11.00 to 15.00.

Best bet for finding out what entertainment is available during a visit is *The Star's* Friday 'What's On' section which has up-to-the-minute details and reviews on stage, screen, cabarets, nightclubs, jazz, records, restaurants, galleries, the arts and even community theatre, plus information on other Toronto happenings, everything from a fashion festival at the Metro Toronto Convention Centre to a Harlem Globetrotters basketball game

at Maple Leaf Gardens. Other sources include the tabloid *Now*, a very comprehensive entertainment guide found on news-stands and in restaurants all over the city, and the monthly listings in *Toronto Life* magazine.

The legal age for drinking in Ontario is 19. Restaurants and clubs serving liquor, beer and wine can be open from 11.00 to 01.00, Monday to Saturday, and from noon to 23.00 on Sundays. Bars and other establishments can be open from noon to 01.00 Monday to Saturday. They cannot open Sundays or holidays.

Sale of liquor, beer and wine at ordinary stores is not allowed. Liquor and wine must be purchased at Liquor Control Board of Ontario (LCBO) stores (though some Ontario wineries are allowed to sell their

Escape from downtown and watch the world go by from the Islands

products at a few retail outlets) and beer must be purchased at stores called Brewers' Retail Stores. Hours vary from store to store, though 10.00 to 18.00 are the basic hours, and none are open on holidays. For individual store hours look up the specific outlet under Liquor Control Board of Ontario or Brewers' Retail Stores in the white pages. Incidentally, there is no such thing as a Happy Hour with reduced price drinks in Ontario. Apparently unhappy with cut-rate competition, some bar owners complained that Happy Hours were loosing hordes of drunks to wreak havoc on the province's highways. There was not a shred of proof of this, no police or accident statistics that supported the contention, but in its puritanical zeal the province promptly did away with the practice. And politicians and other well-to-do citizens can now feel secure as they sip away at their drinks. The streets outside will be safe when they wend their ways home.

Entry Formalities
See Arriving

Guidebooks
One of the better sources of travel books in the city is Open Air Books and Maps, 25 Toronto Street, Toronto, Ont M5C 2R1, tel: 363-0719.
Among the books on Canada that could be consulted by prospective visitors are *The Penguin Guide to Canada* and *Fisher's World, Canada*. The *Rowland Travel Guide to Toronto* contains a number of detailed walking tours which are full of historical information and background. Once in the city the *Stoddard Restaurant Guide to Toronto* can be of immense help in choosing dining spots.

Health Regulations
There are no specific health problems for visitors, nor are any special vaccinations needed, though tetanus shots are recommended, as they are for travel anywhere. Emergency help (ambulance, etc.) can be obtained by calling 911 from any phone, or potentially serious medical problems can be taken directly to the emergency ward of the nearest hospital. Hotel staff or taxi drivers can direct you.
Unless you are a provincial resident, you are not covered

by Ontario's medical insurance plan but you can obtain insurance on arrival from Ontario Blue Cross at 429-2661 or Hospital Medical Care at 961-0666 (toll-free from elsewhere in Canada 1-800-387-4770) among other agencies.

Holidays

Christmas and Boxing Day, New Year's Day, Good Friday, Victoria Day (always a Monday, 24 May or preceding Monday), Canada Day (1 July), Civic Holiday (first Monday in August), Labour Day (first Monday in September), Thanksgiving Day (second Monday in October).

Lost Property

First check the store, hotel, taxi company or public transit authority where the loss may have occurred. If not successful try the police department since any property found on Toronto streets is taken into divisional police offices, then, if not claimed, to a central lost property office. To find out the location and number of the division involved call the central police number 324-2222.

Money Matters

Canadian money is divided into cents and dollars (100 cents) with the notes having different colours to allow instant identification. Two-dollar bills, for example, are orange, five-dollar bills blue and one-dollar bills, a vanishing species, green. No more new ones are being printed and their place is being taken by a golden-coloured $1 coin called the Loonie after the bird

Sculpture on Royal Bank Plaza

depicted on the back.

All banks have foreign currency departments and will exchange bank notes or travellers' cheques, as will many trust companies. Many stores, hotels, restaurants and tourist sites will also take US currency but usually give a less favourable rate than would a bank.

Basic banking hours are 10.00 to 15.00 but there are variations on that which vary not only from bank to bank but from branch to branch so it is wise to check by telephone (listings will be found in both white pages and Yellow Pages). But banks are never open on Sundays or holidays and if you want to change currency then you must do it at your hotel, if possible, or at exchange kiosks at Pearson International Airport or Union Station, which tend to charge a fee over and above the profit made on the actual exchange. For that reason it is sometimes better to exchange money at hotels rather than at exchange kiosks even though the rate at the latter may seem better.

For other monetary transactions credit cards will do, of course, and those ubiquitous automatic banking machines are every-where – malls, shopping centres, street corners, what-have-you. Some are designed to work with international cards, others are less generous.

There is an Ontario room tax of 5 per cent on all accommodation and an 8 per cent sales tax charged on most things you purchase (though at some point the latter tax may be absorbed into the Value Added Tax being introduced by the federal government). You will never see the room tax again but visitors who purchase goods and have them shipped out of the province to their homes or take them out within 30 days can apply for a refund of the sales tax, provided the refund comes to more than $7 and the claim is made within three years of purchase. Ask about the pamphlet/application form at the tourist office and keep your original receipts. Photocopies will not do.

Opening Times

The business day is 09.00 to 17.00 for offices and light industries, with many retail stores open from 09.00 to 18.00 early in the week, from 09.00 to 21.00 Thursdays and Fridays and from 09.00 to 17.00 on Saturdays. But there is no absolute overall pattern. Some stores close on Monday and stay open every evening, some close every day at 18.00, so if there is something you particularly want, go during regular hours or check the closing time by phone. Stores in officially designated tourist areas such as Harbourfront are open on Sundays but most major stores are not. Dining lounges and clubs open at 11.00 and bars at 12 noon. Both close at 01.00. Attractions tend to open at 09.00, 09.30 or 10.00, with varying closing hours depending on the season and other factors. For exact times check the **What to See** section.

Personal Safety

There are no particular hazards except in the general way of a big city, though visitors from

Britain must constantly remember to look left before stepping off curbs and also that vehicles can make right turns at red lights.

A Canadian winter, even in Toronto, is somewhat colder than that experienced by most residents of Europe or parts of the USA so they should remember to overdress on really cold days rather than wear too little. Wear layered clothing so that you can add or subtract as needed. Summer, on the other hand, tends to be pretty hot, and should be approached with caution, suntan oil, wide-brimmed hats and light clothing.

Pharmacist

You will find the pharmacist under Pharmacies in the Yellow Pages telephone directory but in normal Canadian speech he is a druggist and his base of operation is a drugstore. They are numerous, easy to find and sell most of the same products sold in pharmacies in Britain and drugstores in the US. For 24-hour operations see **Emergency Telephone Numbers** above.

Places of Worship

Toronto has always been known as a city of churches and that is as true today as it was 100 years ago, but now there is a little more diversity, as a glance under that heading in the Yellow Pages will soon reveal. There are three crowded pages of temple listings, from Roman Catholic through Christa-delphian, Byzantine Slovak, Baha'i and African Methodist Episcopal to Buddhist and

Muslim. However, for the city's synagogues, look under that heading. Also, most major hotels will have listings of local churches and hours of service.

Police

A Metro-wide police force of 5,000 administers the law within the municipality, aided by a detachment of Royal Canadian Mounted Police working on violations of federal law such as drug smuggling and tax evasion. Highways on the outskirts are patrolled by the Ontario Provincial Police.

All uniformed police wear guns and are empowered to use them but not one citizen in a thousand has ever seen it happen other than on television. Uniformed police on the street and in cars are invariably polite and ready to help visitors with information and advice.

Post Office

Canada is not noted for the speed of its mail delivery but that has not kept the cost of mailing letters down. It takes a 38-cent stamp to move an ordinary letter within the country these days, 44 cents to send it across the border to the US and 76 cents to carry it to Europe. Stamps can be bought at hotels and stores and there are small branch post offices in many shopping malls as well. If you need more than a stamp you can find the closest post office by looking in the white pages of the phone book under Canada Post (it is not a government department any more so stay away from the blue pages at the back of the book). For postal information from 08.00 to 18.00,

Monday to Friday, call
973-5757.

Senior Citizens
Senior citizens pay reduced
admissions at most attractions in
Metro and several hotels offer
special room rates. They can
also buy half-price tickets on
GO trains and reduced fare
tickets (60 years or older) on
VIA Rail. But they will not get a
penny off Toronto Transit
Commission fares. There are
reduced fares for senior citizens
on the TTC but you must live
within Metro to qualify. And it is
not a case of discrimination by
the TTC against tourists. They
will not sell the seniors' tickets
to neighbours who live just over
the Metro boundary, either.

Student and Youth Travel
There is only one hostel in
Toronto that is tied in directly

with the International Youth
Hostel Association (IYHA) and
that is the Toronto International
Hostel at 223 Church Street,
Toronto M5B 1Y7, tel: (416)
368-0207, which also serves as
the local representative of the
IYHA.
It has 180 beds in dormitory and
semi-private rooms, there are
no age limits and its rates
(under $20) cannot be beaten. It
has a kitchen and laundry and a
lounge and the reception is
open from 08.30 to 23.00.
It also runs the Youth Hostel
Travel Agency, which offers
reduced-rate tours and even
discounts on transportation to
the airport and tickets to local
attractions. It shares the 223

*Canadian Mounties 'always get
their man' – but they're always
ready to help visitors, too*

Church Street address with the hostel and you can reach it as well as the IYHA and the hostel at the 368-0207 number.
The Association of Student Councils, 187 College Street, tel: 979-2406, is also an excellent source of information on student and youth travel.

Telephones

Pay telephones cost 25 cents for local calls, which have no time limit. You can talk for ten seconds or an hour and the rate is the same. That applies as well to local calls from telephones on private homes or hotels.
Long-distance (trunk) rates are highest from 08.00 to 18.00, drop 35 per cent during the 18.00 to 23.00 time period and are reduced again (to 40 per cent of the daytime fare) from 23.00 to 08.00, all times being at the point of origin. For calls within Ontario and Québec those 60 per cent discount rates also apply from 23.00 Friday right through Saturday and Sunday to Monday at 08.00. On calls to the rest of Canada and the US the 35 per cent discount applies all day Sunday.

Some useful numbers:
Emergency, 911;
Accommodation Toronto, 596-7117; Canadian Automobile Association (CAA) road emergency service, 966-3000; Canada Customs information, 973-8022; Canadian immigration, 973-4444; GO Transit, 665-0022; Gray Coach, 393-7911; International Youth Hostel Association, 368-0207; Metro Toronto visitors' information, 368-9821; Metro Toronto police information, 324-2222; Taxis, 366-6868, 364-8161 and 363-5611; Toronto Transit Commission (TTC), 393-INFO; Travel Ontario, 965-4008.

Time

Toronto is on Eastern Standard Time in the third time zone west in a country which has six time zones and so, like New York City, is five hours behind Greenwich Mean Time. Newfoundland is one and a half hours ahead of Toronto and Halifax is one hour ahead; Winnipeg is one hour behind, Calgary two hours behind and Vancouver three hours behind. Clocks are moved one hour ahead to Daylight Saving Time the first Sunday morning in April and are moved back on the last Sunday morning in October.

Tipping

Tips of 10 to 15 per cent are expected in cafés, restaurants, bars, taxis, etc.

Toilets

There is a long, long trail a winding between the only two public toilets operated by the City of Toronto. One is at 406 Keele Street and the other at the Cumberland Terrace shopping complex, at 2 Bloor Street West. But take heart, just about every shopping centre, mall and the like has public toilets (known as washrooms) and in desperation you could use a bar or restaurant.

Tourist Offices

Tourist information can be obtained from 220 Yonge Street (tel: (416) 979 3143).

ACKNOWLEDGEMENTS

The Automobile Association would like to thank the following photographers and libraries for their assistance in the compilation of this book.

J. ALLAN CASH PHOTOLIBRARY 36 Church, 46/7 Beaver pond trail, 48 Beaver.

L'HOTEL 82.

MILLER COMSTOCK INC. 6/7 Old City Hall (E. Otto), 34/5 City Hall (E. Otto), 57 Kensington market (W. Griebling), 59 Café (E. Otto), 60/1 Breaded rabbit (M. Saunders), 64 Chinese food (P. Croydon), 67 Pasta (F. Ptazak), 79 At night (E. Otto), 90 O'Keefe Centre (W. Griebling), 104/5 (R. Chambers), 117 Baseball (R. Chambers), 118/9 View (E. Otto).

METROPOLITAN TORONTO CONVENTION & VISITORS ASSOCIATION 19 Black Creek pioneer village, 27 Zoo, 92/3 Limelight Theatre, 96 Caribana, 98 Molson Indy, 98/9 Lion dance, 100 Wonderland, 102/3 Waterfront.

NATURE PHOTOGRAPHERS LTD. 50 Chipmunk, 52 Yellow warbler (K. Carlson), 53 Swallowtail (S. C. Bisserot), 55 Long-tailed duck (P. R. Sterry), 56 Maple trees (A. J. Cleeve).

SPECTRUM COLOUR LIBRARY 8 Skyline, 40/1 Falls at night, 44/5 Canada geese.

ZEFA PICTURE LIBRARY Cover CN Tower (Miller Comstock), 4 Spinnaker, 37 Niagara Falls, 42 Moose, 88/9 Roy Thompson Hall, 120 Royal Bank Plaza.

All other pictures used in the publication are copyright of the AA Picture Library, who commissioned J. Beazley for this project.